To Gareth

xxxx

A History of West Indies Cricket

By the same author
A History of Cricket

Gordon Ross

A History of
West Indies Cricket

Arthur Barker Ltd   London
A subsidiary of Weidenfeld (Publishers) Ltd

ISBN 0 213 16585 6

Printed in Great Britain by
Butler & Tanner Ltd, Frome and London

Contents

List of illustrations

1   Early Days

The Caribbean – golden beaches, crystal water, the sapphire bays, blazing blue skies, the mountains full of trees so lofty that they seem to reach the sky, the singing nightingales, parrots, birds of a thousand sorts, the flamboyant trees with their scarlet blooms, the jacarandas; Sam Lord's castle in Barbados – a splendid plantation house, the eccentric whim of a Regency buccaneer; the spectacular festivals of Trinidad; Guyana's St George's Cathedral with its spire rising over 132 feet above the ground, the exotic fruits of Jamaica, mangoes and passion fruit; the lazy peace of the Windwards; Antigua with a coastline peerless for its rugged indentations and superb beaches; and a great export common to almost every one of these colourful and lovely islands – cricket and cricketers.

The cricketers of the West Indies have won world-wide fame and the highest accolades – Lord (Learie) Constantine, Sir Frank Worrell, Sir Garry Sobers – men of exceptional skill and distinction through a long line from George Headley to Clive Lloyd. Their cricket has been instinctive, symptomatic of the surroundings and the environment in which they taught themselves to play. It has breathed the warm air and soft breezes of the Caribbean; sometimes it has radiated the gaiety of a festival; and always it has emphasised enjoyment – the enjoyment of a game to which the players are totally dedicated. Cricket has become a way of life, of West Indian life, sparkling, joyous; it expresses their moods, the light and shade of life, their determination to assert themselves on their own merits. They have brought to the game of cricket an inbred characteristic of their own, hard competitive cricket, but cricket that sometimes produces champagne bubbles: the cultured cricket of Jeff Stollmeyer, once described as the Palairet of the Lovely

Isles; the merciless ferocity of Everton Weekes, who could massacre any attack; the speed and blood-and-thunder of Wes Hall, all arms and legs in his delivery stride; the mystique of Sonny Ramadhin with his box of conjurer's tricks and a sleight-of-hand that always escaped detection; the one-man cricket team of Garry Sobers, batsman supreme, slow bowler, fast bowler, wicket-keeper, peerless fieldsman, great ambassador; and the modern phenomenon, Clive Lloyd, who hits harder off the back foot than any player in living memory; or the fear-less Alvin Kallicharran, who sweeps fast bowlers, including Dennis Lillee, for six to fine-leg, with the nonchalance of a man tossing away an unwanted banana skin.

In the summer of 1975 the West Indies swept to new heights when they won the one-day Prudential Cup tournament in England, having to beat the Australians twice to do so. Some writers called this 'The World Cup', but without South Africa it could not be. I am sure, however, even had South Africa taken part, the West Indies could have beaten them. This can only be conjecture; we shall never know. But I firmly believe that this West Indies side of 1975 was a fine one. I think they might have beaten all comers in one-day, three-day or five-day fixtures. These players are flexible, adaptable. Their five-day cricket is not spoiled because they play one-day matches well; the side has a depth of batting of varied dimensions and fine bowlers to support it. West Indies cricket teams have scaled great heights in the past: 1950 in England; 1960–1 in Australia with a tied Test Match and a ticker-tape send off; 1961–2, when the West Indies won all five Tests in a series against India; and in 1963 and 1966 they beat England 3–1. Theirs is a story of players who have become legends, of matches which will linger in the memory and be faithfully recorded for posterity, and in the folklore of the game everywhere.

The origins of cricket in the West Indies are obscure, as indeed they are in almost every other country which has taken it up. There is talk of the game having been played there in the 1830s, but the unreliable source of this information is the loquacious Mr Jingle of *Pickwick Papers*, who alleged that he had played cricket 'thousands of times' in the West Indies in

1836. This we may take with a pinch of salt, but we do know that James Lillywhite coached there in the 1860s, and in 1863 games were played between Barbados and British Guiana in the first inter-colony matches. Jamaica, owing to the distance between the islands, was not included in this series, but they will tell you that club games were played in Kingston around 1860.

In 1892–3 Trinidad joined Barbados and British Guiana in the inter-colony games, but it was not until 1895–6, when R. Slade Lucas took an English touring side for the first time to the West Indies, that their cricketers started to take the game seriously. So when in 1896–7 Lord Hawke, fresh from a South African tour the previous year, and Mr Arthur Priestley took separate teams to the West Indies, they were pleasantly surprised to find that Mr Lucas's XI had brought about a vast improvement in the standard of play, and, indeed, Mr Priestley's XI was soundly beaten by three wickets by a combined West Indian side. These tours, incidentally, were under private enterprise, and it was not until 1910–11 that the MCC sent out their first official side.

The first West Indies side to venture overseas arrived in England in 1900. The team won five of its seventeen matches. It was captained and administered by R.S.A. Warner, the brother of Sir Pelham Warner, and the task of selection was probably his most difficult problem. He was obliged to select a side that would give uniform satisfaction to all the islands without offence to any. Players were chosen from Barbados, Demerara, Grenada, Jamaica and Trinidad, and from St Vincent came C.A. Ollivierre, first in a long line of great West Indian batsmen. Ollivierre was so attracted to the English way of cricket that he stayed in England and qualified for Derbyshire.

The party left Barbados on 26 May 1900 in RMS *Trent* and, after a record-breaking voyage, arrived at Southampton on 5 June. They had a couple of days' practice, and came up to London to make the first appearance of a West Indian team in England on 11 June, on the Crystal Palace ground against an eleven collected by W.G. Grace under the title of London

County. It was a very strong side, not surprisingly it won
handsomely, by an innings and 198 runs. The West Indies
team was as follows: S.W. Sproston, G.H. Learmond, C.A.
Ollivierre, L.S. Constantine, P.A. Goodman, P.J. Cox,
W.J. Burton, L.S. D'Ade, R.S.A. Warner, W. Mignon,
S. Woods. The names of Woods and Burton are significant,
for they were to be the first West Indians to adopt cricket as a
profession.

L.S. Constantine had an indifferent match – 2 and 5, and 0
for 24 in five overs, but Sir Pelham Warner wrote in his review
of the tour: 'Constantine hit very finely on many occasions,
and was altogether one of the most useful men. His 113 against
MCC was a dashing and faultless display.' Constantine came
from Trinidad; his son, the great Learie, was born on 21
September 1902. Summing up the tour, Sir Pelham Warner
concluded: 'The weakest points of the team were (1) The
absence of a reliable wicket-keeper, and (2) the bad judgment
that was too often displayed in running. In this last respect they
improved, but in the early part of the tour they were, both
individually, and as a team, the worst judges of a run I have
ever seen.' He concluded: 'Englishmen will be right glad to
welcome another West Indian eleven within the next three or
four years.'

In 1902 B.J.T. Bosanquet, the inventor of the googly, took
an all-amateur team to the West Indies. Bosanquet's own
version of the birth of the googly is that somewhere about the
year 1897 he was playing a game with a tennis-ball known as
Twisti-Twosti. The object was to bounce a ball on a table so
that your opponent, sitting opposite, could not catch it. It
occurred to Bosanquet that if he could pitch a ball which
broke in one direction and then, with more or less the same
delivery, make the next ball go in the opposite direction, it
would mystify his opponent. After experimenting, he managed
to do this. This technique was so successful that he practised
it with a soft ball at stump-cricket, finally with a cricket-ball.
After endless practice in the nets he progressed to success out
in the middle. This success obviously continued in the West
Indies. Bosanquet was the star of the tour; he took 84 wickets

at a cost of 14·53 runs each, and headed the batting with an average of 33·84.

In the winter of 1904–5 Lord Brackley took a side to the West Indies which included the first English professionals to visit the Caribbean. They were Ernie Hayes of Surrey, and G.J. Thompson of Northants. Also in the party was G.H. Simpson-Hayward, who was one of the last under-arm bowlers in first-class cricket. Simpson-Hayward seldom flighted the ball like the normal run of lob bowlers and did not spin from the leg side; in fact he was almost a law unto himself with the speed at which he could make the ball, delivered with a low trajectory, break from the off. This team took their own umpire, J. Moss, but despite this some friction arose out of faulty umpiring at St Vincent. From the West Indies point of view, they could be reassured as to their cricket future by a fine innings of 99 for St Vincent by R. Ollivierre, allied to his superb bowling – he took 7 for 38 and 4 for 19. Ollivierre was the brother of the Derbyshire all-rounder, and at that time was obviously the best West Indies all-rounder. But the best bowling performance of the tour was by Cumberbatch for All Trinidad. The English team were bowled out for 92 and 100, Cumberbatch taking 8 for 27 and 5 for 30, a match aggregate of 13 for 57, with his right-arm, medium-pace action.

A year later a second West Indies team left for England under the captaincy of Major H.B.G. (the late Sir Harold) Austin and he too was to lose his star batsman to English cricket. This was S.G. Smith, a left-handed bat and slow left-arm bowler who qualified for Northants, helped them to gain second place in the County Championship of 1912, played on many occasions for the Gentlemen *v*. Players, and eventually went to New Zealand. The programme arranged for this tour was perhaps slightly ambitious, for it provided formidable opposition, and many of the most difficult games were arranged to take place early in the season without allowing the visiting side a sufficient period for acclimatisation. The tour began for them with a crushing defeat at Crystal Palace, W.G. Grace's team winning by 247 runs, and at the end of the same week the visitors went down to Essex after obtaining a first innings lead of 153.

Subsequent victories over the Minor Counties and South Wales
were offset by defeats at the hands of Lord Brackley's XI,
Surrey, Wiltshire, Hampshire, Kent, the MCC and Derbyshire.
However, they were redeemed by one startling performance in
the closing stages of the tour – a victory over Yorkshire at
Harrogate which caused something of a sensation in cricketing
circles. Admittedly, Yorkshire were not at full strength, but it
was still a quite remarkable feat for the West Indians to bowl
Yorkshire out for 50, Ollivierre taking 7 for 23, and Smith 3 for
27. The West Indians, who batted first, had scored 270 and
did even better in their second innings. P.A. Goodman made
102 not out and the West Indies declared at 305 for 6. Despite a
century by D. Denton, Yorkshire were all out for 263, which
won the tourists an historic victory by 262 runs.

In the last match of the tour the visitors added Northants
to their list of vanquished, Percy Goodman getting another
century, and S.G. Smith taking 6 wickets in each innings, a
performance which no doubt encouraged the Northants
committee to discuss his future with him, and to determine
that it lay with Northamptonshire. Smith was back in West
Indies, however, in the winter of 1910–11, with the first
officially sanctioned MCC team under the leadership of
A.F.W. Somerset of Sussex. By a twist of irony, Smith was the
MCC's leading bowler against his own countrymen. This tour
was memorable, since it produced a tie in the tourists' third
game with Jamaica. It also proved that cricket in the West
Indies was ripening, for this MCC side was not really strong
enough to test the opposition to the full. The start was somewhat shattering. Barbados beat the MCC twice, each time by
an innings, the visitors' scores in their four innings being 93, 91,
139 and 191. Then, after a few successes, Trinidad beat the
MCC twice at St Clair – once by an innings, and once by
7 wickets. On 5 April 1911 history was made when the first tie
was enacted at Kingston, Jamaica. The scores were: MCC 269
and 131, and Jamaica 173 and 227.

The MCC were back in the winter of 1912–13, again led by
Somerset, and again to be subjected to a good hiding by
Barbados, despite the fact that they opened with a score of 306.

Barbados gave the firm reply of 520 for 6, W. Gibbs scoring 129 not out and George Challenor 118. Once again Barbados won by an innings. In the return match the MCC were shot out for 65, of which Albert Relf scored 41. Dramatic cricket, to be sure. Barbados replied with 447, P.H. Tarilton hitting 157, and Challenor another century. The MCC were 246 for 9 in their second innings, but W.C. Smith (nicknamed 'Razor' by Tom Hayward, because he was so thin) and Somerset himself took the score to 372 in a stirring last-wicket partnership before Smith was finally out for 126, to give Barbados a victory by an innings and 10 runs. The MCC won the representative game despite an innings of 77 by R.L. Challenor, a brother of George. Playing for a West Indian XI, Harry Ince of Barbados hit a brilliant 167; here was a left-handed batsman of the very highest quality.

West Indies cricket, nurtured by an irradiant brand of enthusiasm and a personality warmed by shafts of the Caribbean sunlight, was now emerging in its own right. It was, however, soon to suffer a severe blow to its development – the First World War, which stretched grimly through four English summers and halted the flow of cricketers to the Caribbean. West Indians had to pick up the threads again, as did other peoples of the world.

It was not until 1923 that West Indies cricket took its next step forward. Major H.B.G. Austin, captain of the team that toured England in 1906, brought over another West Indies side. Once again, the principal problem which confronted him was selection of the team. There was no board of control at that time, or even a selection committee, so he had to bear the brunt of whatever criticism was levelled against his final choice. With military precision and efficiency he toured the islands on reconnaissance. There was virtually no current form to use as a guide because the inter-colonial games had been washed out by rain, so he saw what players he could, and took verbal recommendations for those he could not weigh up personally. Among the latter was G.N. Francis, a professional of unknown quantity from Barbados. Francis proved to be the bowler of the tour: fast, with a terrifying leap at the end of his run and boundless energy, he played in all the matches and took 96 wickets. In the last memorable match of the tour Francis and John (another speed-merchant) bowled with such venom that H.D.G. Leveson-Gower's XI lost 6 wickets for 19 runs when set to get only 28 to win at Scarborough.

Two other players created lasting impressions – Learie Constantine, a superlative fielder at cover-point, whose father had made a century at Lord's twenty-three years earlier, and George Challenor. The full touring party was made up of the following: H.B.G. Austin (Barbados, captain), G. Challenor (Barbados), G.N. Francis (Barbados), H.W. Ince (Barbados), P.H. Tarilton (Barbados), C.R. Browne (British Guiana), M.P. Fernandes (British Guiana), C.V. Hunter (British Guiana), J. K. Holt (Jamaica), R.K. Nunes (Jamaica) R.L. Phillips (Jamaica), L.N. Constantine (Trinidad), G. Dewhurst (Trinidad), G. John (Trinidad), V. Pascall (Trinidad), J.A. Small (Trinidad). The strength of the side lay in Challenor's superb batting, the very good fast bowling, and fielding that was a model of keenness and energy. Challenor was in a class by himself as a batsman. He had everything – a classical style and aggression, reinforced by a solid, technically sound defence. He scored eight centuries, six of them against first-class sides, and was rated by discerning critics as being among the best half a dozen batsmen in England that summer. Francis was the old-fashioned, orthodox fast bowler, whose one idea was to bowl at the stumps, and he was the key man in an exciting victory over Surrey at the Oval, when a Surrey side, including Andrew Sandham, Andy Ducat, Tom Shepherd, Douglas Jardine, Percy Fender, 'Podgy' Peach and Herbert Strudwick, was bowled out for 87. Challenor followed with a masterly innings of 155 not out in a West Indies total of 305. Challenor scored 66 not out in the second innings when he and Tarilton knocked off the 121 runs needed for victory without being separated. A handsome victory, this, which gave a valuable psychological boost to West Indies cricket. If they could produce players of the quality of Challenor and Francis and Constantine the West Indians would have riches indeed in the years ahead. A disappointment on the tour was Ince, for whom there had been great hopes; his highest score in the first-class matches was 46 and his average 16·56. George Challenor finished the season with a batting average of 51·86, which gave him third position in the English averages behind Patsy Hendren and Phil Mead. This was Patsy Hendren's golden summer – over 3,000 runs and an average of 77·17. That Challenor was close on his heels was testimony indeed to his skill.

In the winter of 1925–6 the first post-war English team went to the West Indies. It comprised fourteen players, six of them amateurs, under the captaincy of the Hon. F.S.G. Calthorpe of Warwickshire, and included such famous names as Lionel Tennyson, Percy Holmes, Roy Kilner, Tiger Smith, Fred Root, Wally Hammond and Ewart Astill. With the exception of a top-class fast bowler the team had all the necessary requirements, and only one match was lost throughout the tour. The batting rarely failed, and Percy Holmes made the top score of the tour, a glorious 244 in Jamaica, while Hammond played an innings of 238 not out in Barbados. The West Indies produced seven century-makers during the tour: P.H. Tarilton, 178 for Barbados; R.K. Nunes (soon to lead the West Indies in their first official Test Match), 140 not out for Jamaica; G. Challenor, 124 for Barbados; M.P. Fernandes, 120 for British Guiana; W. St Hill, 105 for Trinidad; A. Cipriani, 103 for Trinidad; and C.R. Browne, 102 not out for the West Indies. Rain robbed the MCC of an overwhelming victory in the first representative match. They declared with eight wickets down at 597 (Hammond 238 not out). The West Indies replied with 147 and were 21 for 6 in their second innings (Root 4 for 9) when torrential rain settled the matter. The MCC duly won the second representative game which Fred Root had begun by getting Challenor caught and bowled for nought. In the third game the MCC were in peril, when rain proved their salvation as it had done previously for the West Indies. The scores were: West Indies 462; MCC 264, and 243 for 8.

This match was to be the last unofficial one between the West Indies and an English team sent by the MCC. Lionel

Tennyson had so enjoyed his cricket in the West Indies in 1926
that he took a private team of his own to Jamaica in the next
two years with top-class players of the calibre of Ernest
Tyldesley, Percy Fender, Errol Holmes, Phil Mead and E.W.
(Nobby) Clark, but in the summer of 1928, in England, the
West Indies reached their goal, a goal for which they had been
striving with unrelenting enthusiasm – official recognition and
Test Match status.

2 Test Apprenticeship

In 1928 it was recognised that the West Indies had come through their period of apprenticeship. Karl Nunes led the following party on tour in England with a schedule which included three official Test Matches: E.L. Bartlett, G. Challenor, G.N. Francis, H.C. Griffith, E.L.G. Hoad (Barbados), C.R. Browne, M.P. Fernandes, J.M. Neblett, C.V. Wight (British Guiana), F.R. Martin, R.K. Nunes, E.A. Rae, O.C. Scott (Jamaica), L.N. Constantine, C.A. Roach, W.H. St Hill, J.A. Small (Trinidad); team manager, R.H. Mallett. They desperately needed fine weather more than anything else. They needed, too, to be able to put together all their known talents for the game at a time when England were particularly strong. They fervently needed success to mark their coming-of-age, but success eluded them; disappointment enveloped them. They won only five of the thirty first-class matches. Twelve, including the three Tests, were lost – and all of the Tests by an innings. The weather was bitterly unkind to them – West Indian cricketers need to feel the warmth of the sun on their backs before they can burgeon. Catches were dropped by fingers numbed with cold, and eyes were not sufficiently adjusted to the poor light of a melancholy English summer; ground fielding was enthusiastic but the throwing erratic; the batsmen showed fallibility against a turning ball, and were vulnerable to the increased movement through the air and off the pitch, and Challenor, thought to be the lynchpin of West Indies batting, now turned forty, could not recapture his brilliance of earlier days. Constantine, the incomparable Learie, was a shining light, a perpetual-motion cricketer, but this was not reflected in his performances in the Test Matches.

Disappointing, it was true, but this was valuable experience all the same. Seventeen players were too many for a tour, and thus some were deprived of the experience they so badly needed. The other deficiencies were there for all to see. The West Indies were born into Test cricket at Lord's on 23 June 1928. They faced an England side from one of the golden ages of English cricket: Sutcliffe, Hallows, Tyldesley, Hammond, Jardine, Chapman, Jupp, Tate, H. Smith, Larwood and Freeman. The West Indies fielded Challenor, Martin, Fernandes, Nunes, St Hill, Roach, Constantine, Small, Browne, Francis, Griffith. Hallows and Hammond are two of only three batsmen in cricket history to have scored 1,000 runs during the month of May – the other was W.G. Grace. Four batsmen – Bradman (twice), Hayward, W.J. Edrich and Turner – have scored 1,000 runs by the end of May, assisted by some runs scored in April. Hammond performed his feat in 1927, Hallows in 1928, and both were at the peak of their form for this first Test against the West Indies.

The results prior to the Test had been patchy, and had even included a surprise defeat by Ireland. Constantine scored the first century of the tour – 130 against Essex at Leyton. This was vintage Constantine – he hit three sixes and fourteen fours. Pulling and driving with rare power, he looked a tremendous cricketer. He followed with a 50 against Surrey, but the West Indies bowlers had a rough ride in Surrey's second innings, with Hobbs and Sandham in when Surrey declared at 253. Small scored the second century of the tour at Oxford.

The traditional match against the MCC at Lord's was an absolute disaster. During the lunch interval on the first day a thunderstorm burst over the ground and flooded the pitch, which meant that no more cricket was possible on that day or on either of the succeeding two. Constantine took 10 wickets in the match against Cambridge University, and Challenor found some of his old glitter against Northumberland with a score of 146. St Hill hit a century against Durham, and then came the totally unexpected setback against Ireland, when, in the second innings, the Irish number 8 batsman, T.G. McVeagh, scored 102 not out. Constantine scored yet another century against Middlesex at Lord's, part of an all-round performance of outstanding merit. He scored 103 in West Indies second innings, having hit 86 in the first, then took 7 for 57 in Middlesex's second innings, which totalled 136. The West Indies thus contrived a memorable victory. Constantine's 86, out of a total of 107, were scored in less than an hour. When going on for his second spell of bowling, he sent down six overs and three balls for 11 runs and 6 wickets – a deadly piece of fast bowling, five of his seven victims being clean bowled, beaten by sheer pace. His grand finale was to hit 103 out of 133 in an hour with two sixes and twelve fours. Many great deeds have been performed at Lord's, the Valhalla of cricket, in the 160 years of its existence on the present site, but rarely, if ever, can this one-man dominance of a single match have been surpassed. Jack Hearne, in stopping one drive from Constantine, damaged a finger so badly that he could play no more cricket for the rest of the season, just one piece of evidence of the ferocious and irrepressible play of this exuberant cricketer.

Rain washed away any possibility of a finish in the Yorkshire match at Sheffield, and then came an extraordinary game against the Minor Counties at Exeter. The West Indies forced the Minor Counties to follow on. They had been unable to cope with the speed of Francis and Griffith and seemed little better able to do so in the second innings, until Mr A. Lockett came in at number 5 and hit 154 with H.P. Miles, the number 8, who proved an admirable partner in scoring 61. They had thus avoided an innings defeat which had been very much on the cards, but defeat still looked ominous enough. The West Indies were then skittled out for 103, Nunes, the captain, coming in at number 9 to make 16 – the highest score of the innings. This was a shattering psychological blow with only a day or so to go before the first Test. However, Martin and Nunes scored centuries against the Civil Service at Chiswick before the match at Lord's.

When the day arrived the West Indies, of course, needed all the luck that was going, but they began by losing the toss. The view that the Lord's pitch can be difficult for batting during the first hour or so in the morning is legendary, but there are still very few captains who, having won the toss, would not wish to bat on it. Chapman certainly chose to bat, and although Jack Hobbs was prevented from playing because of injury, England made 401, Ernest Tyldesley scoring 122. The West Indies, none the less, had fielded well, and their fast bowlers were never really collared, Constantine coming out best with 4 wickets for 82, and Francis and Griffith taking 2 each. Challenor and Martin got the West Indies away to a flying start in their first innings; they put on 86 for the first wicket. Martin's departure, however, signalled the beginning of an astonishing collapse: 86 for no wicket became 96 for 5, 123 for 7, and they were all out for 177. Nunes, the captain, hung on grimly for an hour and a half in scoring 37. England's principal wicket-taker was not, as expected, Larwood, or Tate or Freeman, but Vallance Jupp, who made the ball turn a lot and took 4 for 37 in 23 overs.

Chapman was now faced with something of a dilemma because Larwood had strained himself and would not be able to bowl if the follow-on was enforced. But he was a buccaneer cricketer; he would attack on all flanks as long as he had two bowlers left, and he had no hesitation in putting the West Indies in again – with dramatic effect. Maurice Tate bowled Challenor for a duck, and 6 wickets were down for 44, 3 of them to Tich Freeman, who trundled his leg-breaks and googlies with much guile and skill. When Freeman bowled Constantine for nought with his second ball 16 wickets had fallen since lunch for 162 runs. At the close of play the tourists were 169 runs behind, with only 4 wickets intact.

The final morning was cheerless; the finish witnessed by only a handful, and yet the last session produced some of the best cricket of the match. The West Indies went down with a flourish. Small and Roach put on 56 for the seventh wicket, and the former, in company with Browne, afterwards shared in a partnership of 47. Small, batting for an hour and a half, enjoyed the distinction of being the first West Indian to score 50 in a Test Match at Lord's. The West Indies lost by an innings and 58 runs, but they had come of age and would profit by the experience.

Time has shown consistently that when a great player is out for nought, someone usually pays heavily for it. After the Test

Learie Constantine went straight to Northampton, where he took 7 for 45 out of the Northants total of 100, scored 107, and then took 6 for 67 to enable the West Indians to win by an innings and 126 runs. Constantine's pace was altogether too much for most of the county batsmen, and on the final afternoon he performed the hat-trick, sending back C.N. Woolley, Walden and Matthews with consecutive balls, dismissing Walden and Matthews for nought for the second time in the match. His century took ninety minutes and included five sixes and twelve fours. This was an astonishing performance. Whatever Constantine did, he did supremely well; could he perhaps have played every instrument in a symphony orchestra? There was no telling what horizons he might have crossed in other walks of life; he was a man of unfettered exuberance, flair and extraordinary ability. They still talk of those two June days in Northampton in 1928; the Constantine legend still lingers in memory, and for those who were there it will linger always.

The West Indies now faced a triumvirate of strength, from Lancashire and Yorkshire to Nottinghamshire – powerful sides, all of them. There were Hallows, the two Tyldesleys, Iddon, McDonald and Duckworth at Old Trafford; Holmes, Sutcliffe, Leyland, Wilfred Rhodes and George Macaulay at Leeds; and George Gunn, Whysall, Arthur Carr, Larwood and Staples at Trent Bridge; and these were talented sides from number 1 to 11. Rain ruined the Old Trafford match, which was inevitably left drawn. At Leeds, George Macaulay plundered the West Indies in their second innings by taking 6 for 30, and they were all out for 58 and lost by 190 runs. At Nottingham the visitors fought back superbly against a Nottinghamshire score of 393. Bartlett hit 109, Hoad and Nunes at numbers 8 and 9 scored 73 and 62 respectively, and the final total was 378. King George V and Queen Mary paid a visit to the ground during the second afternoon, and both teams were presented to them.

Matches followed against Staffordshire, Warwickshire and Worcestershire. Hoad scored 149 not out at Worcester, where the home side's reply was 439 for 2, Gibbons scoring 200 not out, Nichol 104, and Fox 104 not out. It might be added with some significance that Constantine was not playing in this match.

All the same it was a harsh dress-rehearsal for the second Test Match at Old Trafford. At least on this occasion the West Indies won the toss, which seemed an excellent augury and Challenor and Roach batted extremely well. But it flattered to deceive and, as at Lord's, only a little play was necessary on the third day for England to win by an innings. This was Tich Freeman's match – 5 for 54, and 5 for 39. For once, it was not Constantine's; he scored 4 and 18 and took only 1 wicket for 89. Without a major contribution from Constantine, the West Indies were deprived of their main armoury; their 16-inch guns were missing and they were bowled out for 206 and 115 (St Hill's 38 being the highest individual score) and England's 351 was ample for an innings win.

From Old Trafford to Llandudno and an incredible defeat by Wales. The great Sydney Barnes, then aged fifty-two, took 7 for 51 and 5 for 67. A. Ratcliffe, who was still at Rydal School, hit 71, and Wales won by 8 wickets.

There followed matches against Leicestershire, Somerset, Glamorgan and Gloucestershire before the third and final Test of the series, the highlight of these games being an undefeated century by Nunes against Glamorgan.

The third Test saw Jack Hobbs on his own ground, the Oval, and cricketers of all generations know what that meant. Jack would always put on a show for his local followers, and this time he hit 159. Once again the West Indies were beaten by an innings, Larwood, Tate and Freeman taking 18 of the wickets between them, but the England captain, Percy Chapman, had as much to do with the West Indies downfall as any England player – he held four catches in the West Indies first innings, three of them brilliant ones. His first was at short-leg from a full-blooded hit by Martin; for the second, to dispose of Constantine, he ran across from deep mid-on right behind the bowler to reach the ball; and finally came two sparkling catches at second-slip in successive overs from Tate – one wide and almost on the ground with the left hand, and the other almost as wide and low with the right hand. The West Indies did reasonably well to score 238, but England's reply of 438 was formidable enough, and West Indies could muster only

129, Hammond this time picking up three catches. This was the third Test defeat by an innings. Only a few hundred people gathered to witness the finish, but during the three days more than 28,000 paid two shillings for admission.

There was still a string of matches to be played before this tour reached its conclusion – against Sussex at Brighton, Hampshire at Southampton, Kent at Canterbury, the Harlequins at Eastbourne, an England XI at Folkestone, Julien Cahn's team at Nottingham, and H.D.G. Leveson-Gower's XI in the Scarborough festival. Martin hit a brilliant 165 at Southampton, Browne 103 at Canterbury, and Hoad scored centuries in successive matches (145 and 124) at Nottingham and Scarborough.

For the West Indies, this had been an extremely strenuous tour, especially for the fast bowlers. Bowling at their pace, with every ounce of limb and muscle stretched to the limit, had taken its toll by the time September, with its mists and mellow fruitfulness, had arrived. Constantine became the first West Indian to achieve the double – 1,000 runs and 100 wickets – fifteen centuries were scored (Constantine and Hoad leading with three each) and Griffith took over 100 wickets in all the matches together. Had there been specialist slip-catchers in the side, the fast bowlers would have done even better. This and other refinements were to come in due course. Although the English cricketing public had regarded it as a disappointing tour, for the West Indies it had been the first step on their path to fame. In that respect it was success enough.

In the winter of 1929–30 an England side went to the West Indies to play four Test Matches. If the West Indies felt that they had the right to be regarded as a fully fledged Test-playing country, the composition of the English party hardly reflected that feeling. The MCC had already sent a strong team to New Zealand and Australia under the captaincy of Harold Gilligan, and such players as Hobbs, Sutcliffe, Hammond, Ernest Tyldesley, Tate and Larwood were seeking a winter's rest after a strenuous English summer. The Hon. F.S.G.

Calthorpe's party in the West Indies included Wilfred Rhodes, then aged fifty-two, and George Gunn, then in his fifty-first year. The West Indies were embroiled in an inter-island controversy over who should be captain, which was finally settled by each island being allowed to stage a Test Match to nominate a captain from among its own players in the team; thus Hoad led in Barbados, Grell in Trinidad, Fernandes in British Guiana, and Nunes in Jamaica. The series ended all-square with one game each, and two drawn, so it did produce the first West Indies Test win over England, some remarkable cricket, and one great cricketer, George Headley, who joined the ranks of the elite by scoring a century in his first Test. His scores in his eight innings were: 21, 176, 8, 39, 114, 112 (a century in each innings of his first Test series), 10 and 223, producing an average of 87·87. Yet the great Patsy Hendren, a particular favourite in the West Indies, did even better. His scores in the Tests were: 80, 36 not out, 77, 205 not out, 56, 123, 61, 55, making an average of 115·50.

The West Indies bowling was monopolised by the pace-men, Constantine and Griffith, but wickets were much harder to come by than runs, England scoring a massive 849 in Jamaica. The MCC began the tour with two matches in Barbados and scored over 500 in both of them – 513 (Hendren 223 not out), and 560 for 7 (Hendren 211 not out, Sandham 105). Sealy, the young wicket-keeper, scored a century in the first match, and Hoad and Tarilton did likewise in the second.

On 11 January 1930 at Kensington Oval, Barbados, the West Indies faced England in the first official Test Match held on West Indian soil, setting another milestone in West Indies cricketing history. Clifford Roach became the first West Indian to hit an official Test century against England. His 122 seemed sufficient to set the West Indies on the way to a sizeable score at 303 for 3, but at this point the innings collapsed and West Indies were all out for 369. England topped this figure comfortably with 467, of which Sandham contributed an exceptionally fine innings of 152. At this point, for the first time in Test cricket, a new star of radiant brightness emerged and there came the first of many brilliant innings to be played by George

Headley. He added 156 with Roach and 142 with de Caires, thus ensuring that England would have no chance of winning. Derek Sealy, incidentally, who had hit a century off the MCC in the colony game against Barbados and was playing in his first Test Match, established a new record by being the youngest player ever to appear in a Test – 17 years, 121 days. It was a highly promising start.

The second game of the series proved what a great leveller the game of cricket is. It illustrated, too, how the pendulum of fortune swings sharply, first in one direction and then the other. Clifford Roach, who in the first Test had scored 122 and 77, was out for nought, twice – bowled by Voce, and caught Sandham bowled Voce. England, 12 for 3 in their first innings, and 52 for 3 in their second, won by the decisive margin of 167 runs despite having been led in the first innings. For England, it was a three-man triumph: Hendren scored 77 and 205 not out; Ames scored 42 and 105; and Voce took 4 wickets for 79 and 7 for 70. The highest score by a West Indian batsman was 58, made by R.L. Hunte and Constantine. The West Indies gave little indication here of the great events which were to unfold at Georgetown on 21, 22, 24, 25 and 26 February.

It was Fernandes who took the West Indies into this decisive battle in their cricket history. They beat England by the huge margin of 289 runs. Roach and Headley carried most of the batting on their own shoulders: Roach scored 209 (making the bowlers pay for his two ducks in the previous Test), and Headley became the first West Indian to score a century in each innings of a Test – 114 and 112. The fast bowlers, Francis and Constantine, took 15 wickets between them. The consistent Hendren hit 56 and 123, but support for him was almost negligible, except for a last-ditch effort by Calthorpe, who scored 49 and staved off defeat until only a quarter of an hour before the end. The West Indies had shown the MCC that it was no longer any use sending sub-standard sides to the Caribbean. This was a severe setback for English cricket, while Hobbs, Sutcliffe, Hammond, Ernest Tyldesley, Tate and Larwood were resting at home in the English winter, and Duleepsinhji and Woolley were heading the batting averages

of the MCC team in New Zealand and Australia, scoring runs
in profusion.

The West Indies now had a stature of their own; the series
was level and the fourth and last Test at Kingston, Jamaica,
was to be played to a finish. But as rain prevented any play on
the last two days and the England team had to sail for home,
no victor emerged, after an England first innings of staggering
proportions. At one time England were 667 for 3, and finally
finished with 849. Andrew Sandham played a Test innings of a
lifetime, hitting 325 runs. He batted for ten hours and broke
the existing Test record of 287 for England against Australia
set up by R.E. Foster at Sydney in 1903. Ames contributed 149.

Two decisions relating to the match are worthy of reflection. The first was the West Indies decision to drop Learie
Constantine. In his absence, their bowling was massacred.
The second was the decision by Calthorpe not to enforce the
follow-on when England had a lead of no less than 563. Was it
that some of his elder statesmen were tired of fielding after the
West Indies had scored 286? Whatever the reason was, the
decision robbed England of any possible chance of victory. The
West Indies were left with the absurd target of 836 to win, and
were concerned only with survival. As it happened, it was
scarcely a matter of dull defence. Headley hit 223, and when the
tropical rains came and washed the match away, the West
Indies were 408 for 5 and Calthorpe's decision not to enforce
the follow-on became even more of a mockery. There was food
for thought now for the cricketing nations of the world. The
West Indies had awakened from their embryo stages and were
now fully grown as a Test-playing country. Their way to the
stars was signposted; they knew precisely where they wanted
to go.

West Indies cricket was now on the verge of breaking new
ground. In November 1930 a West Indian expedition under
the captaincy of G.C. Grant arrived in Australia. Grant, a
Trinidadian, was a Cambridge blue, and must be unique as a
captain; he had never captained before, and what is more, had

never seen his team play, for he joined them in Australia at a time when Australian cricket was probably at its zenith. The eleven Australian names for the first Test read like a cricketing Debrett: Ponsford, Jackson, Bradman, Kippax, McCabe, Woodfull, Fairfax, Oldfield, Grimmett, Hurwood and Wall. It was not long before Grant had won the respect of his players. In the first Test he scored 53 not out and 71 not out, and also caught Bradman for 4 off Griffith. Grant, incidentally, became the first West Indian player to score a not out innings of over 50 in both innings of a Test Match. Australia, however, won comfortably, Ponsford and Archie Jackson scoring the 172 needed for victory without loss. In Jackson, Australia seemed to have a rising star of exciting proportions; tragically, shortly after midnight on 16 February 1933 Jackson died of tuberculosis.

In the circumstances, the West Indies needed a generous measure of luck to tip the balance in the second Test. They received none. Australia won the toss, batted, and were 323 for 4 at the end of the first day. Rain prevented any play on the second day and completely altered the character of the wicket on the third when play was resumed. Australia lost their last 6 wickets for 46, so difficult were the conditions. In addition, the West Indies were reduced to batting a man short. Bartlett, in catching Kippax from a powerful hit at mid-on, had a finger crushed against his boot and took no further part in the match. The West Indians were bowled out for 107 and 90, to lose by an innings and 172 runs. It was a cruel piece of luck but part and parcel of the game of cricket.

At Brisbane, in the third Test, the rubber was decided. A double century by Bradman, a century by Ponsford and an Australian total of 558 knocked the stuffing out of the West Indies. Headley made a superb 102 not out in a meagre total of 193 in reply, and the team was bowled out again for 148. It was the wiles of Clarrie Grimmett which weaved the main spell of destruction in this defeat by an innings: he took 9 for 145.

At Melbourne, in the fourth Test, the West Indies touched rock bottom on the tour: the match was all over on the second day. They batted on what appeared to be a reasonably good pitch and were shattered by Ironmonger, who came on as first

B

change and took 7 for 23, Headley with 33 being the only West Indian to score above 20. Australia found no such problems in either the pitch or the bowling, and declared at 328 for 8, Bradman hitting 152. In their second innings the West Indies were faring even worse than in their first when Scott came in at number 9 and hit 20 not out, the top score in a total of 107.

At this point West Indies morale must have reached its nadir, and the world and his wife expected them to lose the last Test almost as a matter of course. But resilience is a trait inbred in the West Indian's character. At Sydney the boot was on the other foot. This time the Australians got the worst of the pitch; Grant timed his declarations admirably, scored runs himself in addition to Martin (123) and Headley (105), and his bowlers rallied to the cause, Francis taking 4 wickets in the first innings and Griffith 4 in the second. The West Indies, 350 for 6 declared and 124 for 5 declared, beat Australia (224 and 220) by 86 runs. Although outgunned in the series by four to one, the West Indies had at least beaten Australia as well as England in a Test Match. The players were accorded a very enthusiastic reception on their victory at Sydney. The pleasure which West Indies could give on the cricket fields of the world was beginning to become apparent.

And so to 1933 and another tour of England with the first Test at Lord's and a chapter of disappointments for the West Indies. Learie Constantine was at that time playing for Nelson in the Lancashire League, and they declined to release him regularly. G.N. Francis was the professional for Radcliffe and they allowed him to take Constantine's place in the Lord's Test. Clifford Roach got a pair at Lord's for the second time in his Test career and, having had England 155 for 6, West Indies were beaten by an innings. Their batting was a bitter disappointment, only Headley reaching 50 in either innings. Nearly the whole of the first day was cut to waste by rain, but the match was still all over by four o'clock on the Tuesday afternoon. There appeared to be a substantial difference in the two sides, but once again the West Indies proved their ability to be undeterred by a setback, however demoralising, and Barrow and Headley restored their prestige with centuries in the second Test at Old Trafford, although even so a heaven-sent opportunity was let slip. At one time the West Indies were 226 for 1, but then fell away to 375 all out. This was just one run more than England despite a century by Jardine. Martindale with his fast leg delivery bowled with great determination and effect, taking 5 for 73. The match moved to an inconclusive end on the completion of the West Indies' second innings of 225.

The performance at Old Trafford had given cause for optimism as thoughts turned towards the Oval for the third and final Test. But once again Constantine was not available, and the West Indies faced an England side unique in one respect: for the first time in England's Test history no Surrey player was selected – and at the Oval too. England won the toss and spent the first day compiling a score of 312. Conditions on the Monday were certainly not favourable to the West Indies. There had been a little rain in the early morning, but although this did not affect the pitch to any great degree, the atmosphere remained gloomy, so that against the pace of bowlers of the calibre of Clark and Nichols the West Indians were at a decided disadvantage and they never recovered from a disastrous start in conditions so different from the clear light of the Caribbean. Clark shot out Roach, Barrow and Da Costa, and paved the way for C.S. Marriott, a Kent amateur leg-break and googly bowler, to weave his web of spin. The West Indies were all out in two hours for 100, and followed on. Roach then clearly decided that attack was the best method of defence; he hit a six and five fours and with I. Barrow put on 77 for the first wicket in forty minutes. It was too good to last, and the character of the batting had to be tailored to suit the occasion, but once again the West Indies had no answer for the bag of tricks which Marriott delivered. He finished the match, which England won by an innings and 17 runs, with 11 wickets for 96 – yet he never played for England again !

The West Indies were now having to lean too heavily on Headley and Martindale. Headley, as a batsman, stood out head and shoulders above the rest. Martindale, as a fast bowler, was almost equally indispensable. Headley's fame had preceded him to England and his performances came up to the highest expectations. In first-class matches he made over 2,000 runs with an average of 66, and played seven three-figure innings including one of 169 not out in the second Test in which, supported by Barrow, who also made a century, he added 200 for the second wicket. Nobody in bowling approached Manny Martindale; he had an excellent action, generated and maintained great pace, and took over 100 wickets. The West Indies suffered an injury to F.R. Martin, who strained a leg while chasing a ball at Lord's in the match against Middlesex and played no more cricket during the tour. The best all-rounder was O. Da Costa, but there was a notable lack of top-flight spin bowling in the side, though E. Achong, a left-hander, bowled for long spells with good control, but in a summer of bounteous sunshine he rarely got a pitch to his liking. Some typical English bad-weather pitches could have shown him to be a much better bowler than the tour statistics reveal. Despite Grant's admirable leadership, only five first-class matches were won out of a total of thirty.

Rivalry was resumed in the West Indies in the winter of 1934–5. England sent a capable side, but by no means the best that was available. R.E.S. Wyatt, the captain, plus Ames, Farnes, Hammond and Leyland had all played against the Australians in the previous English summer, and one or two others were on the edge of the Test team, but England was still not sending her best cricketers to the Caribbean and once again paid the penalty; this time outright defeat by two matches to one and one drawn. The West Indies now had an exhilarating trio of speed – Martindale, Constantine and Hylton – and they gave England a rare roasting, claiming all but 17 of the 64 England wickets which fell in the Test Matches. Headley was in masterly form; it was almost automaton cricket as he piled run upon run. In the Test Matches he scored 485 runs for an average of 97, and his 270 not out in the final Test created a new record for the West Indies against England.

The first Test in Barbados still remains one of the most extraordinary ever played between the West Indies and England. On a pitch affected by rain runs were absolutely at a premium, and a hint of things to come was given by Wyatt when he won the toss and immediately put the West Indies in to bat. Ken Farnes, tall, well framed, with a fast bowler's shoulders, was almost unplayable, making the ball lift off a length, and he shot out the first four West Indies batsmen at a personal cost of only 15 runs. Half the side were out for 31. Here was the supreme test for Headley and he showed all his skills as a world-class player on any type of pitch – the true test of greatness. Headley was finally run out for 44. Headley apart, Hylton with 15 was the only other player to reach double figures, and the West Indies were all out for 102, the spin of Hollies and Paine mopping up the tail-enders.

Now it was England's turn, and their performance was almost a replica of that of the West Indies. Hammond scored 43, but all the remaining batsmen failed except Iddon, who was 14 not out at the close, when England were 81 for 5. In this absorbing day 15 wickets had fallen and it was certainly anybody's match. Rain held up the start on the second day until after tea, and when Hylton took 2 wickets in three balls with no addition to the score Wyatt was swift to put the West Indies in again, declaring with the England score still at 81. The pattern of struggle was maintained. Headley was out for a duck and the West Indies lost 3 wickets with their score at 4. Roach, Hylton and C.M. Christiani offered token resistance, but big Jim Smith, the Middlesex quick bowler, was on the rampage. At 51 for 6, Grant took the boldest decision of his life: he declared and left England to make only 73 to win – 73, mark you, with Wyatt, Leyland, Hammond, Hendren and Ames in the side. At 48 for 6 Grant looked a genius. This fantastic Test Match was going the West Indians' way, Martindale bowling faster and faster, in full cry. Wyatt's gambit of opening with two hitters, Farnes and Smith, had failed. Their redeemer was Hammond, who, like Headley, was a master craftsman on all types of pitch. Hammond not only stood his ground but won the match by hitting Martindale for six.

While England had won this match, this was not a fair criterion of the ability of the two sides, for the West Indies might just as easily have won and it was in the lap of the Gods as to who came out on top. But one thing was certain: the fast-bowling trio of Constantine (who had not played in this match), Martindale and Hylton was a powerful attacking spearhead, and if anything was to bring about England's downfall it was this. In Trinidad, for the second Test, Learie Constantine was performing in front of his own people, and what a performance he put on – 90 and 31 runs, and 2 for 41 and 3 for 11. This was a firecracker display and how the crowd responded. It was fitting, too, that the match ended in high drama, England's last wicket falling with the penultimate ball, giving the West Indies a handsome win by 217 runs. Trinidad was in a fiesta mood that night, and for the next few days as well.

England had been severely handicapped by the absence of Farnes, owing to a neck strain, and without him it was rather surprising that Wyatt once again put the West Indies in to bat on winning the toss, especially as nothing like the same conditions as in Barbados were prevailing here. Even so, the West Indies were 115 for 4 and events seemed nicely poised for England. However, Constantine now joined J.E.D. Sealy and the situation changed dramatically. Sealy played polished cricket, scoring in a wide arc, and runs were flowing. Constantine was just being Constantine, and together the two batsmen flourished until at close of play the West Indies were 284 for 9. The following morning Constantine scored all the 18 runs which were added to the total before he was out for 90 with the score at 302. High drama was to follow, drama that was already characterising this series. England were 23 for 5, and once again the fast bowlers were reaching a crescendo. England was in danger of total collapse, but Hendren, Iddon and Errol Holmes picked up the pieces and with brave defiance took the score to 258.

The West Indies now batted again and with consistent though not prolific support for Headley, who made 93, they reached 280 for 6. Grant now declared, setting England 325 to win. Never for a moment did England look like getting anywhere near this score, and only Townsend with 36 could do anything with the pace-men in a situation which seemed inexplicable – Wyatt had reversed the batting order. Of course England's tail-enders were not equal to the West Indian speed-merchants with the new ball, and England were 75 for 6 and without a dog's chance of saving the game. They were all out for 107, with Leyland and Holmes, the last pair, falling almost in the final minute of play. If Leyland and Holmes had batted in their proper places, there was every chance that England would have saved the game. But the fruits of victory belonged to the West Indies, and what they had done once they could do again.

The third Test in Georgetown was undistinguished. In a game of comparatively low scores – England 226 and 160 for 6 declared, West Indies 184 and 104 for 5 – only Wishart, Headley and Wyatt exceeded 50, and no West Indian bowler took more than 4 wickets in the match. The feature of the game was the leg-breaks and googlies of Eric Hollies: he took 7 for 50 in the West Indies first innings.

And so to Kingston, Jamaica, and a match of a very different sort – George Headley's. Perhaps this was Headley's finest hour; he batted for a little over eight hours and hit thirty fours, to score 270 not out. In achieving this he figured in two notable partnerships, that with Sealy yielding 202 for the third wicket, and a stand with Rolfe Grant realising 147, Sealy scoring 91 and Grant 77. The formidable total of 535 for 7 declared was a certain insurance against defeat. The West Indies, therefore, would not lose the series, and they had the rapier thrusts of Constantine, Martindale and Hylton to help them win it. When England were 26 for 4 it was obvious that the West Indies were not to be denied victory, but they were foiled by Ames (126), Hendren (40), and Iddon (54), England reaching a final score of 271. Inevitably, the follow-on was enforced and there was no thwarting Constantine and Martindale this time. England, who lost Wyatt, struck on the jaw by a rising ball from Martindale, caved in altogether and were all out for 103.

G.C. Grant, the West Indies captain, retired during England's second innings with a sprained ankle and Constantine took over the leadership. The win in this match and the first overall triumph in a series must have brought more joy to Learie Constantine than anyone else, for he had witnessed the early setbacks and trials and tribulations, and he had known many problems during his days at Nelson. Now at last the West Indies and West Indian cricketers had crossed to the sunny side of the street; difficult days were behind, great days lay ahead.

Four years were to elapse before the West Indies and England crossed swords again, this time in England, in that fateful summer of 1939, a summer when the possibility of war dominated every English heart and its sombre cloud hung menacingly over the English way of life, and its cricket. The tour began in miserable weather and it ended prematurely as war engulfed Europe, the West Indies losing one Test Match and drawing the other two in a three-match series. But there was a great deal to be said for the West Indies on the credit side. George Headley, who had already scored a century in each innings of a Test Match against England, did so again – this time on the historic turf of Lord's. Jeff Stollmeyer, later to become an integral member of the famous 1950 side, and subsequently President of the West Indies Board of Control, scored a century on his first appearance at Lord's against Middlesex at the age of nineteen. Constantine, now approaching thirty-seven, re-captured all the amazing energy that made him one of the most dazzling cover-points when he first came to England in 1923. Sixteen years later, this amazing cricketer was as exuberant as ever. Rolfe Grant brought the side over, and its members were as follows: R.S. Grant (captain), J.B. Stollmeyer, V.H. Stollmeyer, G. Gomez, T. Johnson, E.A.V. Williams, E.A. Martindale, J.E.D. Sealy, C.B. Clarke, G. Headley, K.H. Weekes, I. Barrow, L.G. Hylton, and H.P. Bayley. They were joined in England by J.H. Cameron and L.N. Constantine. There was plenty of young blood here to blend with the seasoned cricketers. Barrow, the principal wicket-keeper, failed to find his previous form, and after the Lord's Test gave way to Sealy. In contrast to the previous series played in the West Indies, England now had their very best available side in the field.

Of course, the Lord's Test belonged to George Headley, despite Hutton's brilliant 196 and Denis Compton's 120. Headley's century in each innings was another milestone in his glittering career. But this effort proved to be in vain because the sharpness had gone from the West Indies speed attack, the most successful bowler being Cameron. As if to remind the players of what lay ahead, a few thunderclaps rolled about the sky, but did no more than that. England won by 8 wickets.

Rain did play a vital part in the second Test at Old Trafford. Only thirty-five minutes' play was possible on the first day, more rain falling over the weekend and during the later stages of the game. The result was a low-scoring game in difficult and cheerless conditions and with poor light. Grant had put England in, but Saturday's storm had not given his plans any chance to materialise. The fun did not begin until after lunch on the Monday, when England collapsed and declared at 164 for 7 in the face of the cleverly flighted off-breaks of Grant, and the leg-spin of Bertie Clarke. Rolfe Grant clearly knew what the wicket held in store for the West Indies and decided that aggression was the only way to play it. He began by freely cutting Bowes and Copson, and when Tom Goddard appeared, Grant really made the sparks fly. He showed an utter disregard for the imposing array of short-legs and three times hit Goddard for six. He had made 47 out of 56 when Fagg caught him in front of the sight-screen. Headley scored 51, and Sealy 16. As to the rest, they were presents for Bill Bowes, and he took 6 for 33 on his birthday. From this point onwards the game died a death. Rain had cut such deep inroads into the proceedings that a decisive result was virtually impossible, though Constantine managed to pick up 4 second innings wickets.

Thence to the Oval for the third and final Test; a feast of runs. England scored 352 and 366 for 3; the West Indies 498. There were centuries by Hutton and Hammond for England

and by K.H. Weekes for the West Indies. A result was never on
the cards, and the honours were even. When Hutton and
Compton and the West Indian players left the field at the end,
the mood was a melancholy one. This was the last Test Match
to be played until March 1946 – six years and six months of
land, sea and air bombardment intervening, during which
first-class cricket was just a memory. For the West Indies it was
the end of an era. They had played a total of twenty-two Test
Matches, winning four of them, losing twelve and drawing six.
In the eleven years that had elapsed since 1928, West Indies
cricket had been shaping its destiny. It had produced some
exceptional players and some good ones, but to become a real
force in world cricket it would have to produce many more of
them. There was never any doubt that it would. They had been
testing years, these. They represented the positive shape of
things to come; a gentle breeze, then a wind, then a hurricane.
West Indies cricket was already on the wing.

3　Post-War Triumphs

Comparatively, the three Test series which followed cricket's resumption after the war marked the turning of the tide – not an ebb tide, but a consistent flow in one direction. The West Indies, until the outbreak of war in 1939, had lost twelve Test Matches out of a total of twenty-two. In the first three series after the war they lost only one out of thirteen, beating England five times out of eight, with their first visit to India in between, where they won the only finished match of five. The pioneer days were over; work in the hatchery by the early heroes – L.S. Constantine and his son Learie, George Challenor, Percy Goodman, G.N. Francis, Karl Nunes, C.R. Browne, H.C. Griffith, Clifford Roach, Manny Martindale, and the great George Headley had given West Indies cricket a positive shape, a character of its own, as typically West Indian as many of its natural exports from the soil. But then cricket has been embedded in the soil for generations, expressing as it flowers the West Indian way of life in all its fullness.

War affected cricket in the Caribbean islands to a much lesser extent than in the other Test-playing countries, except perhaps India, though many West Indian cricketers joined the fighting forces and saw service in various theatres of war. These were, however, formative years; it was, in a sense, the gathering storm in world cricket. Young players were being developed in the domestic scene of West Indies cricket – names which one day would ring round the world. Clyde Walcott was at Harrison College in 1941; Frank Worrell, a young all-rounder, was at Combermere; and several of these young talents were in a Barbadian side which visited Trinidad in 1941 to play a two-game series after a two-year lapse in major competitive cricket. Trinidad won the second match – the match-winners were the

Stollmeyer brothers. A year later the two teams met again –
Gerry Gomez, John Goddard and a hostile fast bowler named
Lance Pierre playing principal roles in Trinidad's overwhelming victories. In 1942, when Trinidad returned the visit, they
were caught on a brute of a pitch after rain and were bowled
out for 16 by Derek Sealy, who took 8 for 8. Prior Jones was
now bowling very fast; Jeff Stollmeyer made his first double
century; and one by one players who were to form the nucleus
of that great expeditionary force in 1950 were emerging, although, when the war ended, the West Indies had first to pre-
pare for the arrival of an MCC side in the winter of 1947–8, and
two years of feverish activity lay ahead. In January 1946 a
foretaste of what was in store for bowlers of all denominations
and varieties was enacted in Trinidad. Barbados in their second
innings were 45 for 3; at which point Worrell was joined by
Walcott; two-thirds of the famous triumvirate was now being
forged in a piece of shattering and history-making batsmanship.
Barbados declared at 619 for 3. This was merciless hitting.
Walcott established a record individual score for the ground
when the total stood at 461 – hitting 233, Worrell having made
179. Next day the world fourth-wicket record of 502 (held by
Worrell and Goddard) was smashed, and with a great drive to
the boundary Walcott took the partnership to 559, breaking the
555 record for any wicket made by Herbert Sutcliffe and Percy
Holmes for Yorkshire against Essex at Leyton in 1932. When
Barbados declared, Walcott was 314 not out and Worrell 255
not out. Walcott hit five sixes and twenty-five fours and batted
for 348 minutes; while Worrell hit eighteen fours in seven minutes
less time. Trinidad fought back magnificently in this run-feast.
Facing arrears of 671 they saved the game through the combined efforts of Ganteaume, Trestrail and Gomez. Ganteaume
and Trestrail, fighting gallantly, added 207 for the second
wicket – a Trinidad record – Trestrail's 151 being a tremendous
performance for an eighteen-year-old; then Gomez went on
triumphantly to 213 before stumps were drawn and the record
books closed on this quite remarkable match.

The following year two matches between Jamaica and Barbados had special significance. George Headley proved that he

was still a great player: he scored 203 and 57, both not out. A young player named Everton Weekes scored 97; Allan Rae, the son of E.A. Rae, scored 111 and 128, the first time that this feat had been accomplished in an inter-colonial match; and then Weekes hit 123. Both matches were drawn. If England was extending her wartime espionage system into the field of cricket and a proper reconnaissance had been carried out, the talent which abounded in the West Indies would have been palpably obvious. Surely the time had now come for England to send the strongest side possible; lessons of the past should have been learned. England, building her prestige again after the war, needed the moral boost of success anywhere, but once again a side considerably below maximum strength was sent. From the West Indies point of view, they were between the devil and the deep. They had to ask themselves whether the great profusion of runs being scored by a number of batsmen was because the batting was so good it could eclipse any other in the world, or whether it was because there was a scarcity of top-class bowling. Had they fast bowlers at the same speed that had produced so effective an armament in attack in the days of Constantine, Griffith and Martindale, or were they being lulled into a false sense of security by the results achieved in domestic cricket, whereas only the arena of international cricket could be the real yardstick by which to judge their ability? Some thought that England's strongest side would have best answered the question; others took the view that a side just below top class would enable the West Indies to come back to international cricket by degrees. So far, the West Indies had beaten England only three times in seventeen Tests.

The West Indies need have had no qualms over the issue in question. The MCC followed tradition and left at home such players as Compton, Edrich, Yardley, Bedser, Wright and Hutton, ultimately sending Hutton out when this ill-starred venture was desperately in need of reinforcements. The party, well below England's best, was plagued by an unprecedented number of injuries, beginning when G.O. Allen, the captain, pulled a calf-muscle while skipping on the ship's deck on the voyage out and he missed the first three matches in Barbados.

Gubby Allen, a magnificent cricketer, was then forty-five years of age and, never completely recovering from his mishap, found his leadership an arduous undertaking. The result was that for the first time in cricket history, the MCC went through an overseas tour without a single victory to its credit, not even one in the colony games. With Allen *hors de combat*, much was expected of Butler, the other fast bowler, but he ran into a chapter of misfortune: he pulled a leg-muscle in the opening match, developed a serious attack of malaria during the second Trinidad match and broke down against Jamaica. So England's two main bowlers were rarely in action. Laker constantly bore the pain of strained stomach-muscles; Ikin spent several days in a Trinidad hospital with carbuncle trouble which left him somewhat weak; Tremlett complained of strained ribs; Brookes chipped a finger-bone when fielding in the first Test and took no further part in the tour; Hardstaff missed several matches through tearing a leg-muscle; and Place bruised a knuckle in the first Test and ruptured a groin-muscle while hitting a century in the second Trinidad match. It seemed that the war was still on; this was more like a casualty clearing station in the western desert than a cricket team on tour. The West Indies, too, were not entirely free of misfortune. Headley, Worrell and Stollmeyer each missed at least one Test, and Lance Pierre, one of the Trinidad fast bowlers, was not fit enough to appear before his own crowd. Against a crippled attack – with Laker's off-spinning the find of the tour – the West Indies batsmen made hay in the sunshine. They were much too good for an impoverished attack; the real test of just how good they were would have to be deferred for the time being. Frank Worrell scored 472 runs against the MCC in eight innings, including 131 not out in the third Test at Georgetown. Ganteaume, Carew, Worrell and Weekes hit Test centuries, Bob Christiani was out for 99 at Bridgetown, and in total, fourteen centuries were scored against the tourists' bowling, Gerry Gomez hitting the highest score – 178 not out for Trinidad. In the first Test at Kensington Oval, Barbados, the West Indies team was as follows: C.L. Walcott, J.B. Stollmeyer, E. Weekes, G.E. Gomez, G.A. Headley, R.J. Christiani, J.D. Goddard, E.A.V. Williams,

W. Ferguson, P.E. Jones and B.M. Gaskin. They were captained by George Headley, who went in last in the second innings
because of a strained back. The West Indies were poised for
their first post-war Test victory when a rainstorm prevented any
cricket after the first hour's play on the last day. The match was
a triumph for E.A.V. Williams, who joined the side only at the
last minute when Worrell dropped out suffering from food
poisoning. It was a success too (and, in its way, a tragedy) for
Christiani, who was out for 99 in his first Test Match, and thus
missed by one run joining the elite who have scored a Test
century on their début.

The West Indies totally dominated the first day: at the close
they were 244 for 3 and seemingly on the way to a huge total.
But spin bowlers know what a wonderful ally they have in the
rain in the Caribbean. Two sharp showers left the pitch fast and
lively, but not treacherous, and next morning Laker took 6 for
25 in nine overs. The remaining West Indies wickets went down
in an hour for the addition of 52 runs, bringing a total of 296 all
out. By the end of the second day, when England were 150 for
3, the outcome of the proceedings was nicely in the balance –
but not for long. When Robertson (80) and Hardstaff (98) had
been prised out, England's resistance collapsed and they were
all out for 253, giving the West Indies a narrow lead of 43.
England still fought back, this time with the spin of Howorth,
and at 144 for 5 the West Indies were still not in a secure
position. But there now came some remarkable cricket.
Williams, who had bowled well to take 3 for 51, arrived at the
wicket and struck the first four balls he received from Laker for
6, 6, 4, 4. It poses the question as to whether any other player in
a Test Match has begun his innings with two sixes? Altogether,
Williams scored 72 out of the 96 runs added for the sixth
wicket with Christiani in sixty-three minutes. This swung the
pendulum sharply. Rain was still lingering and when England
looked to be in considerable difficulties on a rain-affected pitch
and were 71 for 4, it predetermined their efforts in a more
positive way: rain flooded the ground, and England were able
to scrape out unscathed.

For the West Indies this match set another pattern for the

future. George Headley was captain – the first black cricketer to lead them. Others were to follow him; Frank Worrell, Garry Sobers, Rohan Kanhai, Clive Lloyd. Can any country in the world, it may be asked, boast five Test captains in their history who scored as many runs – and as attractively?

In the absence of Headley and Stollmeyer, Gomez was given the captaincy in the second Test in Trinidad and the West Indies tried a new opening pair – Carew and Ganteaume. Very few Test selectors can have picked two new opening batsmen who scored a century apiece in their first association together. The West Indies were never in danger throughout the game, but few West Indians would want to deprive Billy Griffith, such a popular secretary of the MCC and a true friend of West Indies cricket and cricketers, of the glory he earned the hard way. There are many stories told about this occasion; some true, some to be taken with a pinch of salt. It has been said that Gubby Allen, now fit to lead again having missed the first Test, had such a depleted team at his disposal, that he vowed that the next man to walk through the England dressing-room door would open the innings! It happened to be Billy Griffith. The batsman upon whom England were depending so much was Jack Robertson – in form, and a beautiful player in the true classical mould. He had made 2 when Billy, his unexpected partner, ran him out. Gubby Allen was furious, and Billy has said in jest (perhaps in truth!) that he was so afraid of facing Gubby's wrath that it was safer to stay at the wicket and face the West Indies bowlers. By the time they came off for lunch Gubby's anger had cooled a little, and Billy then battled on in this his first Test Match to score 110 not out at the close, carrying on the next day to reach 140. Surprisingly enough, England were therefore able to reach a highly commendable first innings score of 362. But the West Indies had a trump card too. The new opening pair, Carew and Ganteaume, put on 173 for the first wicket, both, as mentioned, hitting centuries, Worrell followed with 97 and Gomez with 62 to give the West Indies a lead of 135. Robertson, his unhappy experience with Griffith behind him, batted magnificently to score 133. But there was virtually no support for him and England fought to hang on for a draw. Rain helped them by cutting short the play on the Saturday by two hours, leaving the outfield slow. The bowlers were obliged to use towels to dry the ball. The West Indies were finally set to score 141 in fifty-seven minutes. They sent in Weekes and Worrell with the hard-hitting Williams at number 3, as if to try for the well-nigh impossible, but when Godfrey Evans, later to emerge as one of the world's great wicket-keepers, took a brilliant catch with his right hand to dismiss Weekes, it was obvious that the target was beyond human endeavour, and a fascinating game of cricket moved to its close. Despite the prolific scoring W. Ferguson with his right-arm spinners took 11 wickets in the match.

Stricken with injuries, Allen asked the MCC for Len Hutton, who duly flew out and played against British Guiana within three days of arriving; it was a triumphant début; he hit 138 in the first innings and 62 not out in the second. If it was felt that Hutton's magnetic presence would turn the tables in the third Test, this proved for England to be a forlorn hope. The West Indies won overwhelmingly, looking better equipped in every phase of the game, except perhaps where Godfrey Evans was concerned.

The colony match in Georgetown had been abandoned without a ball being bowled, which suggested that the pitch for the Test would substantially help the bowlers. It did, which puts an innings of 131 not out by Frank Worrell in the highest possible category. And the West Indies had found a new captain – John Goddard. Although he failed with the bat twice, as opening partner to Carew, he broke the back of England's batting by taking 5 for 31 and shooting England out for 111 – 186 behind the West Indies first innings score of 297. Goddard had exploited a drying pitch after rain with considerable skill. The follow-on was enforced, but the pitch had been rolled twice and this took much of the spite out of it. England scored 263, leaving the West Indies to make only 78 for victory. They lost Carew, Goddard and Christiani with only 26 on the board, but Walcott and Gomez made light work of the remaining 52 runs needed to win the West Indies a handsome victory.

They were to repeat the performance at Sabina Park, this

time by 10 wickets. The West Indies were set 74 to win in the second innings, almost identically the same target as at George-town, and this time they staged a carnival finish. Goddard and Stollmeyer got the runs in thirty-seven minutes, Goddard hitting a six and eight fours. Twice England had looked to be in a commanding position. Hutton and Robertson put on 129 for the first wicket, but then the side was all out for 227. In their second innings England were 316 for 4, but all out for 336. For the West Indies there were two exceptional performances. Everton Weekes with a superb display of batsmanship and power hit 141 – his first Test century; and Hines Johnson, at the age of thirty-six, and 6 feet 3 inches tall, gave an impressive display of pace bowling to take 10 wickets in the match for less than 100 runs. He looked every inch a fast bowler, yet he rarely bowled a bumper. He pitched the ball well up, compelling the batsman to play strokes; and he beat them by sheer pace, swinging the ball only a little but moving it in off the pitch. 'Is he as quick as Lindwall?' people asked. Some say that he was – and certainly some of England's batsmen will testify that he was quick!

Wisden says of the series: 'On current form, the West Indies must be the strongest cricketing body apart from Australia, and they should be very popular and attractive when they come to England in 1950.' Prophetic words!

Before England in 1950, however, there was India in the win-ter of 1948–9. The first Test Match between India and the West Indies took place at New Delhi on 10 November 1948, the first Test Match to be played in India since 1933–4. It was an astonishing match. Having been 27 for 3 the West Indies made 631 in their first innings, Walcott scoring 152, Gomez 101, Weekes 128, and Christiani 107. With four century-makers, the West Indies thus equalled England's record against Australia at Nottingham in 1938 (Hutton 100, Barnett 126, Paynter 216 not out, Compton 102). More than two days of the match re-mained at the end of the West Indies marathon innings, but Indian wickets are well enough known by bowlers the world over. Admittedly India followed on, but with a massive score of 454, and they had made 220 for 6 in their second innings when the game ended.

For the second Test George Headley was unfit, and so had ended, it seemed, a glittering career in Test cricket. For a very long spell he had carried the West Indies batting; now he could retire from the scene comforted by the knowledge that his example had stimulated many, with the result that the West Indies now possessed a wealth of batting talent. In this second Test, the West Indies again reached over 600. Weekes swiftly followed his century at New Delhi with another even more prolific innings: this time he hit 194. Allan Rae, the opener, scored 104. India, standing at 273 and 33 for 2, were in serious trouble. However, Modi and Hazare and then Amarnath saw them to safety, Modi and Hazare hitting centuries. They finished with 333 for 3.

The third Test at Calcutta belonged unconditionally to Everton Weekes. He made a century in each innings, which gave him a total of five successive Test centuries: 141 against England at Kingston; and four against India – 128 at New Delhi, 194 at Bombay, and 162 and 101 at Calcutta. Already he had established a world record with his flawless technique and unquenchable appetite for runs; he wanted runs like Bradman wanted them, in greater profusion than anyone else could achieve. Walcott hit a century in the second innings of this third Test, as did Mushtaq for India, in the third drawn game of the series.

At Madras it was a different story, the West Indies winning an outright victory by an innings and 193 runs. Rae and Stollmeyer each scored a century in an opening partnership of 239 – a record for the West Indies, beating the previous best of 173 by Carew and Ganteaume against England in 1948. When the second wicket fell at 319 the full glare of the spotlight was turned on Everton Weekes. Could he possibly score yet another century to achieve an astonishing run of six consecutive Test 100s? It looked all the way as if he would. He took a bit of time to settle into his rhythm, but once he had, his batting machinery was seen to be in full working order. Sadly, when 10 runs short of his target, he was run out. This was a big personal disappointment, but the West Indies total of 582 gave their bowlers plenty of leeway. Trim had been given his chance to the exclusion of Atkinson, and how well he took it. Jones, Gomez and Trim gave the West Indies attack a sharp edge, and between them they succeeded in bowling India out twice – in the second innings on a wearing wicket for as little as 144. Trim was the leading wicket-taker with a total of 7 for 76, while Jones took 6 for 58 and Gomez 4 for 95.

This victory virtually meant the winning of the series. With the power of West Indies batting it seemed unlikely that India could achieve a breakthrough, and yet at Bombay in the final Test the West Indies did not bat to their full capacity, even though Goddard won the toss for the fifth time in the series. In fact, the West Indies very nearly lost the match. India, left to score 361 runs for victory in 395 minutes, were 355 for 8 – only 6 runs short of victory – when the game ended, Hazare scoring 122. Sen, India's wicket-keeper, was unable to bat, which meant that India's last pair were at the wicket, so until the very last over the match could have gone either way. This was a splendid Test Match and a credit to the cricket of both sides.

Weekes completed the Test series with a batting average of 111·28, while Stollmeyer's was 68·40, Walcott's 64·57 and Rae's 53·42. Trim, Jones and Gomez took 43 wickets between them. Here was the nucleus of a side to take on anybody; there was no shortage of material in any facet of the game.

So to the winter of 1949–50 and the grouping of the forces for the assault on England. During this period three Trinidadians hit Jamaica's bowlers for 581 for 2, Stollmeyer scoring 261, Trestrail 161 not out, and Ganteaume 147. The Jamaican batsmen had trouble with the spin of Ferguson, and a young right-arm bowler, S. Ramadhin, took 8 wickets in his first match. Barbadian batsmen, too, were in tremendous form – Weekes, Marshall and Walcott all scoring prolifically. Christiani and Pairaudeau were also pressing their claims. It would be not so much a question of who to pick, but who to leave out. The batting, it was felt, could take care of itself anywhere in the world, but it is bowlers who ultimately win matches. Here lay the whole crux of the final selection.

At last the moment of truth arrived and sixteen players were selected for the tour of England: J.D.C. Goddard (Barbados, captain), J.B. Stollmeyer (Trinidad, vice-captain), R.J. Christiani (British Guiana), G.E. Gomez (Trinidad), H.H. Johnson (Jamaica), P.E. Jones (Trinidad), R.E. Marshall (Barbados), L.R. Pierre (Trinidad), A.F. Rae (Jamaica), S. Ramadhin (Trinidad), K.B. Trestrail (Trinidad), A.L. Valentine (Jamaica), C.L. Walcott (Barbados), E.D. Weekes (Barbados), C.B. Williams (Barbados) and F.M. Worrell (Barbados). On paper, the main power of this side was the batting; and pace bowling, on firm pitches. Of the sixteen players, six were essentially batsmen – Weekes, Worrell, Stollmeyer, Rae, Trestrail and Marshall; three all-rounders – Goddard, Gomez and Williams; five were bowlers – Johnson, Jones, Pierre (all fast), Ramadhin and Valentine; and two wicket-keepers, both class batsmen, Walcott and Christiani. Stollmeyer and Gomez were the only members of the team who had toured England in 1939, and these two, with Goddard, Weekes, Rae, Walcott, Christiani and Jones, had also toured India in 1948–9. Only three – Rae, Valentine and Ramadhin – had not played against the MCC in their own season of 1947–8. The manager of the team, as in 1933 and again in 1939, was J.M. Kidney. In England it was felt that the palpably weak link in the side was the spin bowling; after all Ramadhin and Valentine had had precious little experience of first-class cricket. Time was to tell a very different story!

John Goddard was the obvious choice as captain of this side. He was a solid left-hand batsman and a useful bowler of right-arm, medium-paced off-breaks, and it was also said that he was the best fieldsman in the West Indies since Learie Constantine. He had played in nine Tests, seven as captain, without once being on the losing side; at the age of seventeen he had scored 200 in a school match. He hit his first century in big cricket in

1942–3, and in the following year shared in the first of two world-record stands of over 500 for the fourth wicket – 502 unbroken with Frank Worrell, of which Goddard's contribution was 218.

Jeff Stollmeyer was probably the most elegant batsman ever to come from the West Indies. In 1946–7 he scored 324 against British Guiana, the highest individual score in inter-colonial cricket, and he had made three double centuries in first-class cricket. In India he was one of the four leading batsmen with an average of over 60.

Bob Christiani, the only representative from British Guiana, was a quick-footed right-hand batsman who hit the ball extremely hard. He was the reserve wicket-keeper to Clyde Walcott, a fine field, and able to turn a leg-break quite appreciably. He had scored 99, it will be recalled, in his Test début against England at Bridgetown. Christiani was recognised as the best batsman Guiana had ever produced. His career aggregate, number of centuries and average were all records. His brother Cyril had toured England in 1933 as wicket-keeper.

Gerry Gomez, a Trinidadian, was a forcing right-hand batsman and a medium-fast swing bowler. In earlier years he had earned his fame by prodigious batting performances on matting wickets. He had played in all four Tests against England and all five in India. He found that Indian conditions suited his bowling. He took 9 for 24 against the South Zone team – the only instance of a West Indies bowler taking 9 wickets in an innings.

Hines Johnson was in age the senior member of the party – he was thirty-nine and had reached the veteran stage for a fast bowler. He had missed the Indian tour for business reasons, but in the final Test against England had taken 10 for 96 in 65·5 overs, a fast-bowling stint of great merit. His energy would have to be conserved for the vital matches.

Lance Pierre was a surprise selection for the tour to complete a fast-bowling trio made up of Johnson, Jones and himself. Pierre moved the ball both ways at a pace rather quicker than that of Jones but rather less than Johnson's. He had played in the Georgetown Test against England in 1947–8.

Prior Jones was making his second tour, having been one of the pace bowlers in India where he headed the averages with 51 wickets at 18·55. He had a high and easy action off a long run-up. He was the only player in the party who had taken more than 100 wickets in first-class cricket.

Roy Marshall was one of the three opening batsmen and had earned his selection with a sparkling 191 for Barbados against British Guiana. A stylist who would put his full repertoire of strokes on display from the first ball he received, he was later to become an outstanding player in English county cricket with Hampshire.

Allan Rae was the son of E.A. Rae, who had toured England with the 1928 side. A left-hand opening batsman, he was fully conversant with English conditions, having read for the Bar in England for two years, and he had scored prolifically in club cricket for Winchmore Hill and a team from the BBC. His record in first-class cricket was remarkable. He had played only three innings in the West Indies, scoring a century in each innings of one inter-colony match. In India he was one of four leading run-getters, and had shared the West Indies Test record for the first wicket – 239 with Stollmeyer.

Sonny Ramadhin was the mystique man of the party. The youngest player in the team by a few days, he made cricketing history by being the first East Indian to represent the West Indies, and by being one of only two players selected for a tour after their first tournament. In the trials he took 12 Jamaican wickets for an average of 19·25 runs. All that most people knew was that he was a spin bowler – what sort of spin they were to find out (or not find out) as the tour developed.

Ken Trestrail was once known as the 'Boy Wonder' of the West Indies. He began his first-class career as a schoolboy aged sixteen, and scored 85 against British Guiana in Trinidad. He had yet to play in a Test Match, but his upright and aggressive batting style seemed to have all the ingredients for top-flight cricket.

Alfred Valentine, by his selection, had broken a record never likely to be beaten or even approached: in first-class cricket his total bag was 2 wickets for 190 runs. It seems totally incomprehensible that he was considered at all, let alone selected.

Admittedly he had enjoyed great success over a period of two years in his local senior cup competition, but what sort of training was that for bowling against Len Hutton? The West Indies believed that a left-arm spin bowler was an absolute necessity on English wickets, and they believed that Valentine was their man. They showed courage and, as it happened, an absolute stroke of genius!

Clyde Walcott was bracketed with Don Tallon as the leading wicket-keeper of the day, and he was a strong batsman who used every ounce of his powerful frame. He had made his début at the age of sixteen. His driving and pulling had an intense ferocity about them and his scoring had been prolific. He had made five centuries in India, and his tour aggregate of 1,366 was the highest in the side.

Everton de Courcy Weekes – the very name conjures up ideas of cut-and-thrust and dash – was at that time probably the best batsman in the world, having already scored five consecutive Test centuries. He was the only West Indian, George Headley apart, to have scored a century in each innings of a Test Match. In 1940 Weekes had played for Bacup in the Lancashire League.

Frank Worrell had greatly impressed the MCC players in their West Indies tour of 1947–8, as well he might have done – he scored 294 against England in three Tests, at an average of 147. While still a schoolboy he had scored 188 and 68 for Barbados against Trinidad, and in the following season he made 308 not out in the corresponding match at Bridgetown. He had actually made his début for Barbados as a slow left-arm bowler. In 1949 he had played for Radcliffe in the Central Lancashire League, scoring 1,501 runs (average 88·29) and taking 66 wickets (average 17·69). His run aggregate was a league record.

Cecil Williams rejoiced in the sobriquet of 'Boogles' – an appropriate name for a leg-break and googly bowler. He scored his maiden century (108) for Barbados against Trinidad in 1948–9, and in the next match, against the same opponents, he took 6 wickets for 28 runs in the second innings. He pushed his leg-breaks through at a quickish pace, similar in pace to Doug

Wright, though without the loping approach and kangaroo hop which Wright employed in his run-up.

This then was the party, immensely strong in batting on good pitches. Time alone would tell what their ability would be on pitches affected by the vagaries of an English summer, so fickle in its moods and changes of face. The fast bowling seemed the likely spearhead of the attack; the spin bowling, inexperienced and totally untried at the highest level of cricket, was unlikely to make much of an impact on English batsmen, who were so adept at playing spin bowling on their own pitches. However, in retrospect, John Goddard's decision to bring Alfred Valentine was one of the boldest and most brilliant pieces of selection in cricket history. He was quite certain that he must have a slow left-hander for English pitches, and he saw in Valentine's comparative failure ingredients which might blend to create the mixture for which he was looking. Ramadhin's achievements had been only a little better and, in trying to assess the side's potential, English critics took the view that the West Indies were likely to use the slow left-arm bowling of Frank Worrell – or even Williams, if he could find a length with his leg-breaks – and keep Ramadhin and Valentine for the lesser matches or emergencies. If nothing else, it would be valuable experience for them. What happened is now set down in innumerable calypsos.

In one summer's cricket the names of Ramadhin and Valentine sprang from total obscurity to become a piece of history. One talks of them now in the same breath, just as one talks of Grimmett and O'Reilly, or Gilbert and Sullivan, or Burns and Allen, names that are synonymous with each other, indivisible, and each creative – though in very different fields. In this English summer of 1950, Ramadhin and Valentine, both aged twenty, took 258 wickets between them in first-class matches – Ramadhin 135 and Valentine 123– at an average of 14·88 and 17·94 respectively. Of the other bowlers, Gomez took 55 and Worrell 39, the fast bowlers – Pierre, Johnson and Jones – taking only 91 wickets between them. In the Test Matches themselves, Valentine took 33 wickets and Ramadhin 26, Goddard and Worrell coming next with 6 wickets each. These figures show the extent to which this pair of spinners dominated the proceedings. If the question is asked, 'Was this the greatest West Indian side ever?' the answer must be 'No', purely because of the fast-bowling aspect. Put Wes Hall, Charlie Griffith and Garry Sobers (to open with the new ball or first change) into this 1950 side, and you have the greatest.

The batting was as powerful as expected. Thirty-seven centuries were scored (thirty-four of them in first-class matches), Walcott, Weekes and Worrell leading the field – Walcott and Weekes with seven, Worrell with six. In the four Test Matches – each of five days – Rae and Worrell scored two centuries, and Walcott and Weekes one each. But what mattered most of all was that the West Indies won the series by three matches to one, their first Test win on English soil coming at Lord's. Englishmen rejoiced with the West Indies as their supporters danced upon the hallowed turf – sheer joy and elation it was. It was a victory for cricket. For the West Indies it represented a status symbol; they were now world class.

In the Tests, the West Indies used only twelve players. Goddard, whose brilliant captaincy of his team of all-rounders was a cornerstone of its success, not wishing to weaken the batting, used only one recognised opening bowler for each of the four Tests, Johnson playing at Old Trafford and Trent Bridge and Jones at Lord's and the Oval, although Walcott also took over this duty in the second innings when Johnson was injured. For the other three matches Worrell began the attack, bowling left-arm round the wicket at a quickish pace. In fact Worrell shared in England's downfall at Trent Bridge.

Even on bad wickets this side was usually too good for its opponents, and the fielding was a revelation. Weekes, Worrell and Walcott gave the batting an air of uncompromising mastery; for sheer beauty of strokes Worrell was a delight, a sculpture of elegance and artistry; Weekes, shorter, stockier than Worrell, was magical and merciless off the back foot; Walcott, the wicket-keeper, a big man, a sheet anchor, with a sound defence, was capable of handing out vicious punishment to bowlers fast and slow alike.

Events leading up to the first Test ran almost true to pattern, with rain and cold affecting some of the early matches. Yorkshire were beaten on a drying pitch when Prior Jones took 7 for 29, and it seemed that the West Indies reputation with fast bowlers was to be upheld on this tour. Ramadhin took 4 wickets in the first innings but nothing in the second, so scarcely created any special interest. There was a run-riot at the Oval – Weekes scored 232 and Walcott 128 in a drawn game – followed by a remarkable match at Cambridge when the university side scored 594 for 4 declared, David Sheppard making 227 and John Dewes 183 in an opening partnership of 343. The story goes that when the West Indies players reached their dressing-room after the declaration, Everton Weekes was heard to remark, 'Somebody will pay for this.' They did! In the West Indies innings Weekes himself scored 304 not out, Worrell 160, Christiani 111, Stollmeyer 83 and Trestrail 56 not out – an aggregate of 730 for 3. So in the match a total of 1,324 runs were scored for the loss of 7 wickets.

The West Indies themselves fell to spin against the MCC at Lord's, the wily Jim Sims taking 4 for 65 and 7 for 65, and the English team won by 118 runs. Nothing much happened at Oxford when rain prevented any play on the second day and the whole match was contested in bitterly cold weather, and then came three successive West Indies victories at Cardiff, Taunton and Old Trafford. Hines Johnson took 8 wickets in the match against Glamorgan, Ramadhin 6 and Valentine 5. At Taunton the focus was almost entirely on Ramadhin, who took 6 for 57 and 5 for 98. At Old Trafford, however, Valentine burst on to the cricketing scene with a vengeance. After the West Indies had scored 454 for 7 declared, Lancashire were bowled out for 103 and 131. Valentine, in the last game before the first Test Match, and on the same ground, gave a shattering performance. He took 8 for 26 and 5 for 41, a match aggregate of 13 wickets for 67. The pitch became dusty and worn at one end. Valentine had the ability – if not the match experience – to exploit it like an old master. On the second day when 13 Lancashire wickets fell, he took 10 for 43. Here was left-arm slow bowling, with flight and spin allied of the highest class. Was Goddard a clairvoyant? Had his known interest in horseracing bestowed upon him the power to pick 100-to-1 winners? When Valentine had taken 2 for 190 in the West Indies the odds would have been much more than 100 to 1 against his taking 13 Lancashire wickets for 67 only a few months afterwards.

And so to the first Test Match, and for the West Indies disappointment, not least of which was in the pitch itself. Once again their joy was the bowling of Valentine. He took 8 for 104 and 3 for 100 – 24 wickets at Old Trafford in successive matches. Despite this piece of bowling, England won with comparative ease by 202 runs, although when they batted first and were 88 for 5, the West Indies appeared to have achieved a decisive breakthrough. Trevor Bailey (82) and Godfrey Evans (104) retrieved the position, which was precarious, and enabled England to reach a total of 312. For a time it appeared that the almost impossible was possible and Valentine would take all 10 English wickets in the first innings. When the England score was 22 Hutton received a painful blow on the hand from Johnson and was compelled to retire. One run later, Valentine was set in motion. He found the turf so responsive to his quickish left-arm spin that in seventeen overs before lunch he took 5 successive wickets for 34 runs. Fielders near the bat snapped up the catches like vultures swooping on unsuspecting prey; only Bailey, with the dogged dropped bat, and Evans, showing a refreshing touch of aggression in scoring his first Test century, had the answer to him. When Valentine caught and bowled Evans, Hutton resumed. But he, too, became a victim of Valentine, as did Laker, which brought Valentine each of the first eight wickets. However, his now famous colleague deprived him of a world record, Ramadhin nipping in to pick up the last two wickets. Yet while Valentine may not have made statistical history, he certainly made a name for himself.

The West Indies were put out by the spin of Berry and Hollies for 215, giving England a lead of 97. England replied with 288, leaving the West Indies the unlikely task of scoring 386 to win on a pitch which had been so much in favour of spin. As it was, only a classical display by Jeff Stollmeyer prevented a rout; his innings of 78 was a masterpiece in difficult conditions. Only an hour's play was needed by England on the fourth day, and in this time the last 6 wickets went down for 61 runs. The West Indies were well and truly beaten. The loss of Johnson, who pulled a muscle in his side in his first spell, and bowled only two overs in his second (he did not field after tea and was unable to bowl again in the match), was of course a great handicap to them. Walcott took his pads off and bowled, Christiani put the pads on and kept wicket, but this was a spin bowlers' pitch after all, and was unlikely to have been of much use to Johnson even had he been fit.

In between the first and second Test the West Indies recognised batsmen were in prolific form. Weekes scored 279 against Nottinghamshire at Trent Bridge, Rae 179 and Stollmeyer 198 in an opening partnership of 355 against Sussex at Hove – the biggest partnership for any West Indies wicket in England. At Lord's Goddard once again played only one pace bowler: the injury to Johnson had forced a change and Jones came in to replace him. The West Indies won the toss and with Rae as the sheet anchor, and Worrell and Weekes each exceeding 50, they compiled a total of 326, of which Rae's 106 was one of the most valuable centuries he ever made. The pitch seemed true enough and there was no apparent reason why England should not come within reach of this score, or even pass it, but it was here that Ramadhin and Valentine emerged as the fearful destructors of English batting. England were all out for 151, Ramadhin taking 5 for 66 and Valentine 4 for 48. This was finger-spin at its best; the collapse was total and, in a way, inexplicable. Hutton and Washbrook put on 62 for the first wicket and the pitch was true. But cricket is the most fascinating game in the world and perhaps its greatest virtue is its glorious uncertainty. England, 62 without loss, capsized to 122 for 9, and only by Wardle's domination of a brave last-wicket partnership were they able to reach 151. The West Indies, quite unexpectedly, found themselves with a first innings bonus of 175 runs. They owed it all to 'Ram' and 'Val' who bowled with the guile of seasoned performers: they pitched a tantalising length, bowled straight, and found enough turn to beat the bat: Ramadhin spread confusion – no one, by reading his hand, could work out what to expect.

When the leg-spin of Jenkins accounted for the early batsmen in the West Indies second innings it did stimulate food for thought about the pitch. Weekes, Walcott and Gomez, however, dispelled any lingering doubts about it. Walcott and Gomez put on 211 – a record stand for any West Indies Test wicket in England. When Goddard declared, leaving England the highly improbable target of 601 to win, with nearly two days in which to survive, Walcott was only one short of the highest score by a West Indies player in Test cricket in England – 169 not out by George Headley in 1933. Walcott swept and drove with a regal touch; Gomez was the admirable foil.

England in reply produced a piece of batting mastery by one player – Cyril Washbrook. Almost single-handedly he parried the West Indies bowlers for five hours and a half in an innings of resolution and relentless concentration in which he used all the technical know-how which had made him such a great player. He hit one six and fourteen fours, but permitted himself very few liberties against bowlers who were beginning to weave some sort of spell of magic over the English batsmen as few bowlers in the past had done. Valentine was orthodox, Ramadhin highly unconventional – a little man, as Tich Freeman had been. Perhaps it was the high trajectory of their deliveries which caused some of the problems, but there was much more to it than that. England started the last day with 6 wickets left and 383 runs required to win. Ramadhin yorked Washbrook, who failed to add to his overnight score of 114 and that was the end. Wardle struck a few more blows as he had done in the first innings, but no other batsmen offered a challenge and the West Indies won by 326 runs, a victory of staggering proportions. It set the cricketing world alight; the mood of fiesta swept through the Caribbean islands; West Indians in England sang and danced; the calypso writers were busy pounding out 'Those two old pals of mine, Ramadhin and Valentine'. 'Those two old pals' had taken 18 wickets in the match at a little over 15 runs per wicket; they had spun on a Lord's pitch which had given them little encouragement. Exciting cricket it was. Had Ramadhin produced some mystery ball, the art of which no other bowler had discovered in all the years that

cricket had been played? Was there something special about
the physical construction of his fingers which enabled him to
manipulate a cricket-ball in some unique way? Ramadhin was
the topic of conversation not only in English dressing-rooms
from Taunton to Middlesbrough, but in barbers' shops, bus
queues, billiard-halls and back gardens as the third Test at
Trent Bridge was eagerly awaited.

In the meantime, West Indies batting flourished and the side
suffered no defeats between Lord's and Nottingham. Weekes
made 246 not out and Marshall 135 against Hampshire (was
this the innings which predestined Marshall for Hampshire?),
Worrell 159 against Lancashire, and Christiani 130, and Marshall 99, against Northants. Then Marshall scored 188 (what
tremendous form he was in), Worrell 241 not out, and Weekes
200 not out in a score of 682 for 2 declared against Leicestershire. The bowlers during this period were comparatively quiet
except in devastating snatches. Pierre took 8 for 51 and Valentine 7 for 57 in the defeat of Lancashire by an innings and 41
runs; Ramadhin and Valentine shared 17 wickets in the match
against Leicestershire; and Goddard was the leading bowler
against Derbyshire.

The Trent Bridge pitch, notoriously a beauty, where George
Gunn and the Hardstaffs had reaped such rich harvests, lived
up to its great traditions. It was no place for bowlers and the
West Indies did incomparably well to bowl England out for 223.
For a change, it was not so much Ramadhin and Valentine as
Johnson and Worrell, the opening bowlers; they took 6 between
them, Ramadhin and Valentine 4. Rae and Stollmeyer gave
West Indies a sound beginning, putting on 77 for the first
wicket. This was a light bombardment in preparation for the
devastating assault that was to follow, in which Worrell scored
261 and Weekes 129. Records were smashed one after another,
milestone after milestone flashed by, the most notable of which
were as follows:

The West Indies score of 558 was the highest total in any Test
    against England and the highest total by either side in
    England.

Worrell's 261 was the highest Test score ever made at Trent
  Bridge and the highest individual score by a batsman for
  either country in a Test in England.
The fourth-wicket partnership of 283 was the highest stand for
  any wicket made by either side in this series.
The partnership was also the highest Test stand made for the
  West Indies anywhere.
It was the highest fourth-wicket partnership for the West Indies
  in England.

England's batting, on such a wicket as this, was not caught
napping a second time. Simpson and Washbrook put on 212,
Simpson being run out at 94, after which Washbrook soldiered
on to his second century in successive Tests. Parkhouse, Dewes
and latterly Evans carried on the fight to reach 436, a splendid
performance in a second innings, but it was not nearly enough
to save them. The West Indies needed only 102 to win and Rae
and Stollmeyer polished these off between them. Ramadhin
and Valentine together took 8 of England's second innings
wickets, but this time they had to pay a much higher price for
them – Ramadhin taking 5 for 135 and Valentine 3 for 140.
But they still took 12 wickets in the match. At Trent Bridge, on
a pitch which batsmen would like to carry round with them all
summer, this was still a creditable piece of bowling.

Now the West Indies were one up in the series with one to go
– to be played at the Oval. English cricket was given a fillip at
Edgbaston in the match before the final Test when Warwickshire beat the West Indies by 3 wickets – the only county side to
beat them throughout the summer. The West Indies were
bowled out in their first innings for 156 by a thirty-six-year-old
fast-medium bowler, Charlie Grove, on a greenish wicket. He
took 8 for 38. Warwickshire scored 284, West Indies replied
with 222 in their second innings, leaving Warwickshire with
only 95 to win. It was a rare struggle on what can best be
described as a sporting pitch, but the county side managed to
scramble home. Fifty thousand people saw the match: what a
magnet for crowds this West Indies side had become.

To all intents and purposes the West Indies had won the

series at the end of their first innings at the Oval. They scored 503 and by no stretch of imagination had England the slightest hope. Rae and Worrell scored centuries, Gomez making 74 and Goddard 58 not out. England's innings, as it had been at Lord's, was dominated by one great player. This time it was not Cyril Washbrook but Len Hutton, and he carried his bat for a superb 202. This was vintage Hutton – the supreme master on all types of pitch. Compton, who was run out for 44, was second highest scorer. England followed on and were totally destroyed; once again by Ramadhin and Valentine. Valentine took 6 for 39 (10 wickets in the match), and Ramadhin 3 for 38. Victory was achieved by an innings and 56 runs; and victory in the series by three games to one. This was decisive enough to dispel any thoughts about begrudging the West Indies the full fruits of their labours. Their batting had had prolific results; their spin bowling had been a powerful piece of armoury; their fielding was exceptional; the captaincy outstanding; and only their fast bowling fell below the high standards they had set themselves. John Goddard must have been the happiest man in the world. His selection of Valentine for the tour had been a gamble, and the result of it must have surpassed his wildest dreams. Goddard was a shrewd leader; as an all-rounder himself he epitomised the great strength of the West Indies in world cricket – then as now – their ability to produce outstanding all-rounders. It is this which makes team selection so much easier, and the team so much stronger. The year 1950 set a pattern; it was the ideal mixture for continued success.

c

4   Harder Times

The fifties had begun on the crest of a wave with the convincing overthrow of England. Yet if there was a belief that the West Indies now had a world-beating side this was not to be confirmed during the next decade. Australia was the great stumbling-block. In ten Tests during the fifties the West Indies won one, Australia won seven and two were drawn. England were not such easy meat again either. In the next fifteen Tests the West Indies won two, England six, and seven were drawn. It was even a struggle against Pakistan, which ended four to three in the West Indies' favour with one drawn. The West Indies' only overwhelming superiority was over India, with four matches out of ten won and six drawn, and secondly New Zealand, against which they won four, lost one and drew one. So out of forty-nine Test Matches during the rest of the fifties the West Indies won fifteen, lost seventeen, and drew seventeen.

The fact that world cricket was not all plain sailing was to be brought home to the West Indies on their first tour after England – in Australia. They lost four out of the five Test Matches in the 1951–2 series. Why did they do so? What happened to their famous batsmen? How was it that after crushing England the West Indies were beaten so decisively? The averages themselves tell the story in bare statistics, and they are helpful in any kind of post-mortem. Gomez headed the Test batting averages with 36; the famous combination of Worrell, Weekes and Walcott were down the field, Worrell averaging 33·70, Weekes 24·50 and Walcott 14·50. Only Worrell and Stollmeyer scored Test centuries – Worrell 108 and Stollmeyer 104. There was no fast bowler to make any impression in the Tests, Gomez and Worrell were behind Valentine as the leading wicket-takers, and Ramadhin's figures were tragic – 14 wickets at a cost of 49·64 runs apiece.

To begin with, Test cricket since its inception has proved immeasurably that a side with good fast bowlers will always beat a side without them. Australia had Lindwall and Miller; West Indies had no one in the same street. Perhaps the best commentary on the situation is to be read in the Australian Test bowling figures. Their pace bowlers sent down 453·7 overs, and the spin bowlers 195; the pace bowlers took 66 wickets, and the spinners 23. The West Indies could use only what they had brought with them – medium-pacers and spin – and their most dreaded fears had come to pass: after wet summers every season since the war, spin bowlers were at last faced with Australia's traditional shirt-front wickets. Ramadhin found a dusty pitch at Brisbane and bowled well, deserving much better figures than he achieved. At Sydney, he found something like smooth concrete, and had a nightmare of a match, taking 1 for 196. Valentine, however, against overwhelming odds, never seemed to lose his composure, and philosophically accepted the fact that Australian pitches were very different from those in England and that he would have to cut his suit according to his cloth. Valentine was a prodigious finger-spinner, so that even in conditions entirely opposed to his trade he could turn the ball a little; when conditions favoured him, he spun sharply. He had absorbed much of Jack Mercer's teaching: that when things were against him, he must keep the ball well up, use flight and a variation of pace and keep attacking the stumps – and never give up. Valentine improved his reputation enormously as a result of this tour; few others did.

The West Indies were also learning for the first time how Australian cricket is played – with toughness, uncompromisingly, no quarter being given, and free of rash strokes. Test cricket is no place for the adventurous stroke that has a risk attached to it. The opening partnership of Rae and Stollmeyer, which had burgeoned in England, never got off the ground in any Test, because, although Stollmeyer hit a century and 50, Rae had most depressing figures – 0, 25, 17, 9 (he did not play in the third and fourth Tests), 11 and 25. As always happens with a struggling side, fortune seldom smiled upon them: Weekes suffered a severe leg-muscle injury; Walcott had his nose broken and was badly troubled by a displaced cartilage in his spine. But in all these trials the sterling performances put up by Gomez cannot be overpraised. Gomez would have got into any world eleven at this time, although a strict examination of his powers would have tended to lead one to underestimate them. He was an immensely popular cricketer with friend and foe alike; spectators, too, had the highest possible regard for this genial man.

Having spoken of West Indies problems and deficiencies we would do well to remember that one side often plays as well as the other allows it, and this was a very useful Austalian team; it had speed, spin, a wealth of batting, and a keeper playing in his first series who was soon to establish himself as world class – Gil Langley. In fact, in this, his first series, he was responsible for 21 dismissals and equalled Herbert Strudwick's record for a Test rubber. Yet despite the forebodings, the West Indies did win a Test Match and were only narrowly beaten in two of the others – by 3 wickets and 1 wicket – and had they fielded a good deal better they might have turned both these defeats into victories. Some thought it hard on them that the tour itinerary provided for only one state match to be played after their arrival, before the first Test; it seemed a totally inadequate period of acclimatisation They lost to Queensland at Brisbane by 10 wickets and were then pitched into the first Test on the same ground

The West Indies made only one change from the team which had won at the Oval in 1950, Roy Marshall coming in for Jones, which obviously strengthened the batting, but deprived the side of a fast bowler. If bouncers were to be used then the West Indies had no retaliatory measures at their disposal.

It turned out to be a comparatively low-scoring match – the West Indies scoring 216 and 245, and Australia 226 and 236 for 7, and, with the exception of the heat-wave match of 1932–3, this was the first Test Match to be played at Brisbane without any interference by rain. The result changed the thinking of the Australian cricket public very little. Ramadhin and Valentine had caused problems – they each took 6 wickets, and for a time, the Australian batsmen had treated them with a reverence usually reserved only for the old masters. What had surprised the Australians was the West Indians' fielding: five catches were dropped off Valentine within the space of half an hour, after which many a bowler of less stature would have called for his floppy hat and gone straight into retirement! Goddard showed his hand in that his entire faith was pinned on Ramadhin and Valentine, by taking the new ball in Australia's second innings, rubbing it in the dirt, and handing it to the spinners to carry on as before. Greater faith in Worrell and Gomez might have paid dividends; holding catches certainly would have done. So although the West Indies were one down, honours were not too far off from being even.

Jones was promptly brought back for the Sydney Test to provide one spearhead of fast bowling to the exclusion of a batsman – Marshall. Surprisingly, Hassett put the West Indians in. He was gambling on the state of the pitch, for rain had seeped under the covers during the night and conditions looked much more conducive to bowling than to run-making. The West Indies took up the gauntlet thrown down by Hassett and with Worrell making 64, Walcott 60, Christiani 76 (a superb innings) and Gomez 54, they reached a total of 362. Now came the real challenge to the West Indies spinners: there were no friendly qualities for bowlers in the pitch here as there had been at Brisbane, it was every man for himself. Gomez and Jones shot out Archer and Morris for 27, and the visitors were cock-a-hoop. But then followed one of those incidents which, while often occurring in cricket, sometimes become, because of the context in which they take place, a talking-point for a life-time. Prior Jones bowled a bumper to Hassett, the ball passing well over over his head. The Australian captain waved his bat aloft in something of a drum-major's twirl, probably no more than facetious acknowledgement of the ball's elevation, but – his hand touched it. Walcott shot up his left glove, half gathered the ball, and then it dropped to his chest. He got two hands to it now and clasped it to his body but it evaded his clutch and he fell to his knees, finishing flat on the grass with the ball beside him. The bird had flown. Hassett had then made 7; he stayed to score 132, Miller hit 129 and Australia's total was 517. The

West Indies could manage only 290 in their second innings and
Australia knocked off the required number of runs with 7
wickets in hand.

This was a crisis point for the West Indies. Their fielding had
been poor, some of their batsmen had thrown away their
wickets with injudicious strokes, and Ramadhin had taken such
a pounding that his confidence might be in jeopardy.

What lay in store at Adelaide was a most extraordinary Test
Match. From the moment that it was announced that Hassett
would not play, owing to the development of a hip injury, the
first day presented a series of shocks which did not subside until
the last ball was bowled in the evening. Morris, who took
over the leadership, won the toss and Australia batted. They
were all out for 82. The West Indies, in their turn were all out
for 105, and Australia had scored 20 for 2 when stumps were
drawn. So twenty-two wickets had fallen for a total of 207
runs.

Wisden is quite emphatic that a rain-affected pitch made
batting conditions very difficult, but another report says that the
most the groundsman and the batsmen themselves could dis-
cover wrong with it was a damp patch at the cathedral end, and
a ball pitching there was apt to hang fire. Some said that the
batting would have won no prizes in a competition, but could
twenty-two Test players be out in one day if there was nothing
wrong with the pitch? Surely not. And if we accept the fact that
the root cause of the trouble was the damp patch at the
cathedral end, how do we explain the fact that of the twenty-
two wickets that fell on this first day, ten succumbed at the river
end, with which even the most disappointed batsman could find
no fault however hard he tried? Let us just call it 'Cricket's
Mystery Day'. Worrell, bowling with a collection of vultures
crouching on their haunches close enough to the batsman to
pick his pocket, took 6 for 38, and Bill Johnston 6 for 62.

The second day was the day before Christmas Eve. Play was to
continue on Christmas Day, the first time that Test cricket had
been played on this occasion. It was to be a wonderful Christmas present for the West Indies. Australia were bowled out for
255, with Valentine taking 6 for 102. The West Indies were 141

for 4, but Gomez, of the stout heart, and Christiani, were still there to see them to 233 for 4 – and victory. The West Indians had played not only with their heads in this match but with their hearts too. It was a notable achievement and an enormous boost to their morale.

How near the West Indies came to being all-square in the series after the fourth Test will be known only to those players who were involved, and for the West Indians it became a bitter memory of lost opportunity. When Australia's last pair came together on the fourth day Australia needed 38 runs to win; as forlorn a hope as makes no difference. It so happened that they got them – and the West Indies were 3–1 down with one to go instead of level. Ramadhin had not allowed his experiences at Sydney and Adelaide to unnerve him; he bowled well; so did Valentine; so did Trim; and Worrell got a century. It was all very nearly enough, but Ring and Bill Johnston carried the flag for Australia when their number seemed up. Yet it was Hassett's century which made all this possible. This was a great Test Match and the final scores were: West Indies 272 and 203; Australia 216 and 260 for 9. West Indies had lost the match, but not their dignity or reputation. But they had lost the series.

The first day of the final Test contained all the dramatics of the first day at Adelaide. It began not by an announcement that the Australian captain would not play, but that John Goddard would not lead the West Indies and was standing down in favour of Stollmeyer. The reasons given for Goddard's absence were varied, obscure and conflicting. This time 19 wickets fell on the first day, but there were no damp patches; instead the temperature was 105 degrees in the shade. Perhaps this time it was too hot for batting! Gomez and Worrell bowled Australia out for 116, Gomez taking 7 wickets for 55. What a magnificent tour he was having. But the West Indies found that joy and tears can be very close together. They were 64 for 9 at the end of the day, and all out for 78 next morning – Miller taking 5 wickets for 26. By generally consistent batting (four of their players made scores in the sixties) Australia reached 377 in their second innings, from which point onwards the match became virtually a one-man show, Stollmeyer scoring 104 out of the

West Indian total of 213. The final stages were marred by Lindwall's persistent bumpers to Weekes which even caused an outcry from the pavilion, where many members were furious at the use of this form of attack, and there were also outbursts from the Australian cricket writers who described the tactics as inexcusable. The West Indies, at one time 147 for 2, lost 7 wickets for 24 runs in a procession that changed the game from a serious challenge to sheer pathos.

It was a sad ending to the tour, sad especially for John Goddard; the high winds from the Caribbean had blown only in fitful gusts. Before their journey home, the West Indies played two matches in New Zealand, winning one and drawing the other, rain on the last day saving New Zealand from a second defeat after the West Indies had scored 546 for 6 declared (Stollmeyer 152, Rae 99, Weekes 51, Worrell 100 and Walcott 115), Ramadhin and Valentine enjoying themselves to the full. It was cricket with the tension off; and now it was time for reflection and thought about the future.

India's first visit to the West Indies in January 1953 seemed unlikely to provide any major upset, although India did rather better than might have been expected, losing only one Test and drawing the other four. The West Indies had some problems sorting out Gupte, India's leg-break and googly bowler. He took 50 wickets on the tour, only 7 less than those obtained by the rest of the bowlers put together, and 27 of them were taken in the Tests. The wiles of Gupte, however, scarcely impeded Everton Weekes, who finished with a Test batting average of 102·28 after hitting centuries in the first, third and fifth Tests – 207, 161 and 109. Walcott scored 125 in the fourth and 118 in the fifth, and Pairaudeau 115 in the first; Stollmeyer was 104 not out in the third, and Worrell 237 in the fifth. India began the first Test at Port of Spain by scoring 417 (Umrigar 130) on an easy pitch that looked full of runs. The West Indies replied with 438. India totalled 294 in the second innings and the West Indies 142 for no wicket, the game ending in a draw.

The second Test was the decisive one of the series, the West

Indies winning by 142 runs. Stollmeyer, on winning the toss, decided to bat on turf affected by rain, and with Walcott's 98 the West Indies scored 296. India encountered Valentine at his most frustratingly accurate; they were all out for 253. The West Indies managed 228 in their second innings, setting India a target of 272 runs to win. A piece of Ramadhin magic put paid to them, the little master taking 5 for 26, clean bowling Hazare, Umrigar and Ramchand – a considerable feat. India were all out for 129.

Three more Tests followed – and all three were drawn. In the first of them the West Indies were set to make 327 in 165 minutes and not surprisingly gave up the ghost. Weather played the major part at Georgetown – when Walcott scored his first Test century on West Indian soil – and a draw became inevitable when the weather reduced play to one hour on the last day. The fifth Test was notable for the double century by Worrell and five other centuries – Roy 150, Umrigar 117, Manjrekar 118, Weekes 109, Walcott 118. In a match of massive scores – India 312 and 444, West Indies 576 and 92–4 – the West Indies were asked to score 181 in 135 minutes, and being one up in the series considered the chase hardly worthwhile.

The next touring team to visit the West Indies was England, for a series which engendered controversy, rancour, and caused one English cricket writer to refer to the whole affair as a 'cricket cauldron'. There is never smoke without fire; indisputable facts cannot be swept under the carpet – the bottle-throwing at Georgetown after McWatt had been run out, for instance. It is also true that some English players were subjected to pressures the likes of which they had never encountered before on or off a cricket field, but judgement cannot be given in a court of law without all the evidence on both sides being heard. But in any event the series finished all-square at two matches each and one drawn; possibly fate was making its own judgement!

It was a tour of remarkable and sometimes inexplicable happenings. With all the talent that was available to the West Indian selectors, a decision to bring George Headley back into

the Test arena at the age of forty-four was so beyond rational
explanation as to make people delve for rather complicated
reasons – for instance, were there political undertones? Whatever the thinking that motivated his inclusion, and this was the
West Indians' own domestic business, the cricket world was sad
to see him come back and fail. Boxing has so often proved that
soundest piece of sporting philosophy – 'They never come back.'
In the first Test of the series George Headley played for the last
time; in the fifth, Sobers played for the first time, at the age of
17 years, 245 days – as a left-arm slow bowler. With Gerry
Gomez's career in Tests moving towards its close, the rise of
Denis Atkinson, as an all-rounder, was particularly significant.
Denis Compton thought that Atkinson was the most difficult of
all the West Indian bowlers. But still the backbone, the whole
vertebrae of West Indies Test cricket, was Worrell, Weekes,
Walcott, Ramadhin and Valentine. Jeff Stollmeyer was proving
himself an admirable captain, a painstaking tactician, cool
and resolute whatever the situation.

There were two special factors concerning the English party:
they were the first England team to travel overseas by air; and
they were the first to be led by a professional captain – Len
Hutton, whose handling of this tour was beyond reproach.
From first to last, no batsman compared with Hutton. His
performance in leading the Test averages on either side, with
96·71, was overshadowed only by the mastery he showed of
every bowler in every innings of any length. In concentration
and certainty he stood alone, and, when inclined, he produced
his most majestic attacking strokes, without ever allowing the
wine of them to course to his head. In the last three Tests
Hutton's average was a shade under 150 – a masterly performance.

The West Indies played their best cricket in the first two
Tests. Deterioration set in through two batting failures in
British Guiana, and after the draw at Trinidad another collapse
in the first innings of the last Test gave England the surprise
chance they had hoped for but had scarcely expected. The West
Indies bowling suffered because of Valentine's injury and loss of
form, but the belief that bowlers who hunt in pairs are entirely

interdependent was not confirmed in this series. Ramadhin emerged as the most successful Test bowler in either side, taking 23 wickets. The next best by a West Indian was 8.

The West Indies side for the first Test in Jamaica included five players who had not played in the final Test at the Oval in 1950. They were M. Frederick, J.K. Holt, G. Headley, C. McWatt and E. Kentish. Headley's inclusion had been made possible, presumably, because Worrell was unfit. The story of the match in a nutshell is that after the West Indies had made 417, and Ramadhin, Valentine and Gomez had bowled England out for 170, Stollmeyer did not enforce the follow-on, and was booed repeatedly by his own followers for the decision. The West Indies finally declared at 209 for 6 in their second innings, and when England were 277 for 2 it looked as though Stollmeyer had backed the wrong horse. But total collapse followed. Kentish took 5 for 49 and England were all out for 316, to give the West Indies victory by 140 runs. The captain was right after all. There were incidents directed against the umpire Burke, presumably for giving Holt out leg-before when the local hero was within 6 runs of a century in his first Test. Lock was no-balled for throwing, subsequent events proving that there was little wrong with this decision. After shaping well in the matches before this first Test, England's mediocre performance surprised even the West Indians.

In the second Test in Barbados the West Indies were 25 for 3, and Weekes was not playing. England, it seemed, was swiftly redeeming her good name, but here Clyde Walcott took the stage with the total dominance of the principal tenor in the opera *Carmen*. He pulverised England with an innings of 220, Pairaudeau scoring 71 and Atkinson 53. Thus 25 for 3 became 383. Ninth out, Walcott hit one six and twenty-eight fours in his first double century in Test cricket. There were a few sore fingers about among the England fielders.

England's reply was an old, old story, the story of Ramadhin and Valentine. Ramadhin took 4 for 50 and Valentine 3 for 61, and England were 181 all out. Hutton had battled pretty well alone for 72. This whole innings was close to the nadir of English batting in Test cricket; it was grim, faceless cricket, mistaken in concept – the concept of totally committed defence, and attrition. England tried their own patience to the limit – and went beyond it, and in the end got themselves out. Hutton defended every inch of the way for four and a half hours and then surrendered to a reckless stroke, as if he could stand it no longer. Perhaps the attitude of the crowd had affected him, although with a player of his experience it should not have done so. On the third day England scored 128 runs in 114 overs. It is surprising that any crowd remained; it is no wonder that they became restless. England had handed the West Indies the initiative and it was gratefully accepted by 'those two old pals of mine, Ramadhin and Valentine'.

There was worse to come for England. Holt played superbly in a massive innings of 166. Worrell, now fit again, supported him admirably, and the West Indies were able to declare at 292 for 2. It presented England with the daunting total of 495 to get to win. In these circumstances attrition was more acceptable than in the first innings but as it happened England improved incomparably on their first innings performance, as Hutton, Compton, May and Graveney batted – probably under different direction of policy – with much more composure and more like themselves, free of the artificial cricket which was foreign to the very soul of every one of them. Yet despite their efforts England once again collapsed irretrievably and inexplicably, nose-diving from 258 for 3 to 316 all out. If there was consolation – and there can be very little when you are two down after two matches in a five-Test series – it was that Valentine had been beaten, which proved to be the beginning of the end for him in this series, though his partner continued to carry the torch for him. Valentine failed to take a wicket and had 87 runs hit off him in England's second innings. In the next Test he took 1 for 109, after which he was gone for the series. Injury, loss of form, or any other reason, cannot diminish his exceptional talents, Alfred Valentine of calypso fame. But more was to be heard of him yet.

The third Test in British Guiana, whatever its merits as a game of cricket, and it contained many, will live in memory as the 'bottle-throwing Test'. To impartial observers the choice of

Christiani for the West Indies may have seemed surprising, but it does underline one problem which has beset West Indies cricket since R.S.A. Warner selected the first team to come to England in 1900: his choice had to give uniform satisfaction to all the islands without giving offence to any. This has remained an underlying theme in a group of islands so different in their way of life that each island has its own national pride, its own heritage, its own cricketers. On this tour it had been Headley for Jamaica; Kentish in Jamaica but King in Barbados; Christiani for Guiana. Of course the selectors are charged with the duty of picking the best available team and this they do, but island pride has always been an important issue, a situation perhaps not fully understood outside the Caribbean. If, for instance, the British Lions played a match at Murrayfield and not one Scot was included in the side, Scotland would be up in arms. As the West Indian is, by nature, more expressive than the Scot (except, perhaps, when England are at Murrayfield!) it is sensible to try to understand him, and the way he cherishes his own soil. And in this group of islands it is so very different from any other.

The West Indies can seldom have been more confident of success against England than they were when the third Test began. England were two down and had looked like losers, and few West Indians anyway had heard of Pudsey – that piece of Yorkshire granite that breeds a toughness into its sons as hard as the grey stone walls that wind their way through mile after mile of undulating Yorkshire countryside. Herbert Sutcliffe, and now Len Hutton. Hutton, his batting nurtured in the country's best academy – Yorkshire; his leadership, thoughtful; he commanded quietly, almost as imperceptibly as he scored his runs at Georgetown. In this third Test he showed all the qualities of a leader in rallying his men in adversity, and rallying them by the best possible method – personal example.

Hutton won the toss for the first time in eight Tests, and that was one distinct moral advantage. When Watson and May were out for 12 apiece the advantage had wavered a little. The story of the rest of the innings, which rose to 435, is principally Hutton's. After Graveney had gone for 0 at the fall of Compton

for a fine 64, the rest of the side from Wardle down to Statham
gave their captain admirable support. Hutton, in his own words,
'soldiered on', to score 169. He knew all about batting for a long
time and survived for seven and three-quarter hours. When
Alfred Valentine bowled Jim Laker he became the youngest
cricketer to take 100 Test wickets, though this particular
innings had been hard work for him. Ramadhin, however, had
bowled magnificently for 67 overs, with only 113 runs scored
off him and 6 wickets – Watson, Hutton, Graveney, Wardle,
Bailey and Lock, an impressive collection.

The most decisive period for England in the whole of the tour
came in a spell of less than an hour before lunch on the third
morning, when the West Indies were batting. Some say that
Statham's bowling during this period was the finest ever seen
from an England fast bowler. Worrell, opening in place of Holt,
who had not fielded since he pulled a leg-muscle on the Wednesday, sparred at a ball outside the off-stump and was caught
by Evans off Statham at the wicket. Statham, with the breeze
over his left shoulder, now knocked Stollmeyer's off-stump out
of its socket, the ball pitching on the middle-stump and moving
away. Statham then crowded Walcott with Hutton and Bailey
only a yard or two from the bat, and presently Walcott edged
a ball into his stumps endeavouring to repeat an earlier stroke
when he had hit a glorious boundary through a line bisecting
Hutton and Bailey. Statham had taken 3 for 12. History alone
can judge whether this was one of the finest bowling performances by an England opening bowler, but one fact is indis-
putable: it could never have come at a more crucial time in
England's Test history. At 31 for 3 the rains came, making no
more play possible that day.

Weekes, McWatt and Holt were the saviours of the West
Indies cause on the fourth day – a day marred by crowd
incidents, deeply regretted by West Indian officials, who had
nothing but praise for the outstanding leadership shown by
Hutton in standing his ground in an ugly situation and probably,
by doing so, preventing a deterioration. The West Indies, with
Weekes in command, appeared to have repaired the cracks in
their innings, but at 132 for 4 (a notable improvement on 31 for

3) trouble emerged out of a clear blue sky; Gomez played on to Statham; Weekes, when only 6 runs short of what had looked to be an inevitable century, was beaten by a beautiful ball from Lock; Atkinson, fighting for survival for half an hour without scoring, was out to a brilliant caught-and-bowled by Lock, and suddenly the score had slipped downhill to 139 for 7. At this point McWatt and the injured Holt fought a gallant rearguard action and, just when the partnership was on the brink of adding 100 – it was only 1 run short – McWatt went for a second run that would have done the trick. But a pick-up by May and a throw into Evans's gloves ran McWatt out by a yard or more, and McWatt, knowing that his number was up, just kept on running. Ramadhin had arrived at the wicket to replace him when a barrage of bottles was thrown on to the field of play behind the square-leg umpire – there were hundreds of them. Bottles were then thrown in other parts of the field. As officials and police set about restoring order after the game had been stopped, Hutton, bravely and defiantly, waved his players back into their fielding positions. 'We needed the wickets,' Hutton said afterwards. 'This was a match we had to win.' And win it England did. Hutton enforced the follow-on when the West Indies were all out for 251 and then bowled them out a second time for 256, to win by 9 wickets. After the reprehensible incidents enveloping the match (as a game of cricket alone it was a memorable match) it was something of a relief, and it brought a pleasing finale, that England's win was received with creditable sportsmanship and good humour.

The connoisseurs, who knew all about the pitch at Port of Spain, Trinidad – a jute-matting pitch on which no Test had reached a definite finish since it was laid down in 1934 – were as certain of a draw as they were of night following day. No less than 1,528 runs were scored while only 25 wickets fell – an average of over 60 runs a wicket, the bowlers assuming the role of paid work-horses. The West Indies, needing only a draw to make sure of not losing the rubber, batted until just before lunch on the third day and made their highest total in Test cricket – 681 for 8 declared. For the second time in their careers, Weekes, Worrell and Walcott scored centuries in the same

innings and Weekes and Worrell created a record partnership
for any wicket in an England *v.* West Indies series with a
stand of 338. England were handicapped when Statham pulled
a rib-muscle on the first morning and could not bowl again on
the tour, but even he could have found little solace in the conditions prevailing for bowling here. It will suffice simply to list
the principal scorers – Weekes 206, Worrell 167, Walcott 124,
May 135, Compton 133 and Graveney 92 – and give the final
score; West Indies 681 for 8 declared and 212 for 4 declared;
England 537 and 98 for 3.

At Sabina Park, Kingston, Jamaica, Hutton lost the toss for
the fourth time in the series, demolished the West Indies
immensely powerful batting – they were all out for 139 – and
then scored a double century himself to give England a spring-
board from which they were able to win the match and draw
the series. It was an unexpected but quite outstanding achievement. There was no Statham this time to stage an early thrust,
but one was staged all the same. This time the hero was Trevor
Bailey, a cricketer of immense resources and talents. This time
West Indies were 13 for 4, Bailey having prised out Holt,
Stollmeyer and Weekes, while Trueman had dismissed Worrell.
Bailey, at this point, had taken 3 for 5 – yet had Statham played,
Bailey would not have got the new ball. Walcott staved off total
disaster – his side could have been out for under 100 without
him – by scoring 50, but Bailey was picking up wickets all the
time and finished with 7 for 34, a magnificent performance of
controlled bowling. And it was a true wicket, make no mistake.
Sobers, playing in his first Test and batting at number 9, was
14 not out, the first of many occasions when bowlers the world
over couldn't get him out!

Hutton carried the England batting on his shoulders – or at
least half of it. He scored 205 out of 414. King, who had
delivered rather too liberal a supply of short-pitched balls,
though he had bowled well, strained a leg-muscle, and could
not bowl again in the England innings. For concentration and
control Hutton's feat can have had few peers in the game's
long history: he batted for almost nine hours. It was the first
double century scored by an England captain on a tour

abroad and Hutton's nineteenth Test century. When the West Indies first 4 wickets – 3 to Trueman, who produced some of his most accurate and hostile fast bowling of the tour – were down for 123, visions arose of an innings defeat, but Walcott hit a century and Gomez and Atkinson served him well. England needed only to make 72 to win, and they did so for the loss of only Graveney.

This had been a dramatic come-back. When the West Indies were two up after two Tests, and the world was able to reflect on their performances against England in 1950, none but the great optimists would have backed England to have levelled the series. Why did the West Indies allow this to happen? Well, it is hardly a fair assessment to suggest that the West Indies did let it happen; it happened because England improved incomparably during the tour, many of their players reaching their known form mid-way through the tour, and they were good players too. The West Indies had only limited bowling resources to stop them, especially fast bowlers. Kentish and King had bowled well at times, but a look at the Test Match bowling averages will show Ramadhin as the absolute centre-piece. He took 23 wickets, King and Atkinson coming next with 8 each. And it is bowlers who win matches!

The Australian tour to the West Indies in the following winter of 1954–5 was a major success. It was the first Australian tour on West Indian soil, and the Australians won three Test Matches, drew two, and lost none. This meant that the West Indies had now played eight consecutive matches without winning one – the last three against England, and these five. From the Australians' very first practice forty-eight hours after the conclusion of their ninety-six-hour journey, they seemed to cast a hoodoo spell over the West Indies with a regimented display of net practice and fielding, hitherto strange to West Indian eyes. That 52 was the highest opening partnership of the Test series for the West Indies gives an idea of the power of Australia's attack. It was not just Lindwall and Miller, but Benaud (what a joy to see a spinner top the Test Match bowling

averages), Ian Johnson and Archer, and there was not a great
deal wrong with their batting either, especially the irrepressible
Neil Harvey, who finished with a Test average of 108·33,
followed by Miller with 73·16, McDonald with 64·14 and Archer
with 60·66. For the West Indies, it was a wonderful series for
Denis Atkinson – third in the batting averages with an average
of 44·42 behind Walcott and Weekes, and top of the bowling
with 13 wickets (the next best was 6 by Sobers). Tom Dewdney
took 5 wickets, but there was no pace of sufficient quality to
offset Lindwall and Miller. During the series a record number of
twenty-one centuries were scored, and the Australian batsmen
hit twelve of them – also a record.

From the moment that Harvey and Miller began the Test
rubber with centuries it was, with the exception of the third
Test, to be a thoroughly rough ride for bowlers. But the tour
was not without notable events for the West Indies. Collie
Smith scored a century in the second innings of his first Test
Match, prompting R.S. Whitington, the Australian cricket
writer, to comment: 'I have attended the birth of another
Bradman.' What a terrible tragedy when this popular West
Indian was killed in a motoring accident in England. Walcott
hit a century in each innings of the second Test in Trinidad, and
Denis Atkinson and Clairmonte Depeiza (in only his second
Test) shared in a seventh wicket stand of 347 in the fourth Test
in Barbados to take the score from 147 for 6 to 494 – Atkinson
219, Depeiza 122. In the final Test, Walcott did it again, hitting
a century in each innings in a match of fantastic scoring, in one
innings of which one Australian scored a double century
(Harvey, with 204), and four others hit centuries – McDonald
127, Miller 109, Archer 128 and Benaud 121, in a total of 758
for 8 declared. Benaud's volcanic eruption was the fastest Test
century for two years – seventy-eight minutes.

Australia set the pattern for the tour in the first Test. They
declared at 515 for 9, and bowled the West Indies out for 259
and 275 to win by 9 wickets. For Walcott, who made a century,
this was the beginning of an astonishing tour, in which he
scored the following: 108, 39, 126, 110, 8, 73, 15, 83, 155, 110.

Collie Smith's performance was a remarkable one. Twice, in

this, his first Test, he was called upon to face a desperate situation. At one point in the first innings the West Indies were 101 for 5. However, Smith took them to 239 for 6 before he was dismissed, having made 44. In the second innings it was a grim battle for survival. In this situation Smith scored his first Test 50 in seventy-four minutes, his century taking him three hours and twenty-five minutes. He hit fourteen fours in a beautiful innings that was all radiance and flair and infectious enthusiasm.

And so to Trinidad for the second Test. The West Indian selectors left out the injured Frank Worrell, brought in McWatt for Binns, dropped Atkinson and restored Stollmeyer to the captaincy. Sobers, who up to the third Test was believed to have appendicitis, returned. So popular were the Australians that the gates were closed before the start of play on the first day, and it was estimated that the crowd was in the region of 28,000 – the biggest ever to watch a match in the West Indies. However, when the official figures were published, they showed that some 10,000 short of that figure had actually paid; others obviously had found alternative methods of admission – or someone couldn't count!

The story of the match, true to Trinidadian traditions, was runs galore and a drawn game. The West Indies scored 382 and 273 for 4, and Australia 600 for 9 declared. Walcott hit a century in each innings – 126 and 110, while Weekes was only 13 runs short of achieving the same feat when play ended. He scored 139 and 87 not out. Weekes completed an astonishing hat-trick in Trinidad. In his last three Test Matches on the ground he had scored 207 against India, 206 against England and now 139. After rain had limited the first day's cricket to an hour and a half, Weekes and Worrell, scoring 242 together, established a new record stand for any West Indies wicket in a Test Match with Australia. Weekes, with a six and twenty-four fours, gave a scintillating display.

This first Test in Trinidad to be played on a turf pitch was again utterly dominated by batsmen. Australia's first three batsmen hit centuries – McDonald 110, Morris 111 and Harvey 133. At one time Australia were 328 for 2 and the West Indies tried nine bowlers – only Weekes, apart from McWatt the wicket-keeper, being denied a bowl.

The sun was warm, the clouds were high in the sky and there was a faint suggestion of a breeze from west to east when the Australians took the field for the third Test at Georgetown. The pitch, upon which the groundsman Badge Menzies had spent so many devoted hours, looked, and was, perfect; there might be life early on, but then there should be in any good Test pitch. The bonhomie of a beautiful morning, however, was soon, like a chameleon, rapidly to change its colour: the West Indies lost 4 wickets for 52 and only Weekes sustained them for the rest of a very mediocre innings. He was the only stanchion; there was no other visible means of support, and, against all reasonable expectations, the West Indies were put out for 182. Benaud, with his tantalising leg-spin, finally prised Weekes out, and then mopped up the tail to finish with 4 for 15 in 3·5 overs.

Australia began well, adding 71 for the first wicket and at one stage they were 135 for 1. The West Indies appeared to be letting the game drift from their clutches, but the bowlers plugged away and achieved a notable breakthrough. In fact, had not Benaud followed up his bowling by some equally productive batting (he scored 68), Australia could have been in serious trouble. As it was, they reached a total of 257 which gave them a lead of 75. Atkinson and Sobers each took 3 wickets and Depeiza had a particularly good first Test Match behind the stumps, getting a couple of victims and not conceding a bye.

The West Indies fared only a little better in their second innings than in their first. Weekes was out for a duck, after which Walcott and Worrell carried the fight between them, but the home side was all out for 207, leaving Australia to make 133 to win. This they did for the loss of only 2 wickets. The West Indies second innings was a triumph for Ian Johnson and Gil Langley; Johnson taking 7 wickets for 44, and Langley, sharing in the dismissal of five batsmen in an innings, equalled the record of his fellow-countryman Bert Oldfield.

Now to Barbados, of which Alister Macmillan has written:

Warm, favoured lands that never know the biting northern cold,
Where endless summer ever reigns with glories manifold,

And through each tempered shining day and mystic silver night,
The bubbling wells of life o'erflow in streams of deep delight.

The Australians drew this fourth Test at Bridgetown, and in
doing so they won the series to go two-nil ahead, with one to
play. But in West Indian folklore the game abides as a living
legend – the legend of Atkinson and Depeiza. The Australians
scored 668 to make the series as safe as houses. In reply, the
West Indies were 147 for 6; seldom can their fortunes have
touched a lower ebb in a Test Match. Then came Atkinson and
Depeiza to write a piece of history. Together they swelled the
total by 347 to establish a world record for the seventh wicket,
beating the 344 by K.S. Ranjitsinhji and W. Newham for
Sussex against Essex at Leyton in 1902. That both Miller and
Lindwall had hit centuries for Australia and Archer 98, was
indicative of the top quality of Australia's all-rounders, but
even these three with the assistance of a new ball were unable to
disturb Atkinson and Depeiza. While Atkinson looked for the
runs, Depeiza, an admirable foil, girded his loins as Trevor
Bailey did on so many occasions, and entrenched himself. On
and on they went. Depeiza in his 90s received three successive
bumpers from Miller, and while all eyes were upon him
anticipating his maiden Test century, Atkinson was approaching 200. Depeiza finally chopped a ball through gully for four
and he was there. Now the world seemed to stand still. Atkinson
was poised on 199 for what seemed an eternity, and then –
there was a strong element of luck about the decisive run – he
got an inside edge to a delivery from Lindwall and the ball
ran down to Favell at fine-leg. The pair saw the day out, as they
had begun it, at the crease; they now had 307 runs to their
credit for the day's play. A crowd gathered outside the pavilion;
a collection had brought in 1,040 West Indian dollars for the
heroes. The West Indies were now 494 for 6, but still 25 runs
away from the follow-on, but nobody seemed to care about that.
This was Atkinson's day – the golden Atkinson, with the gallant
and cheerful Depeiza providing the silver lining.

It was all anti-climax the next morning. Depeiza was bowled
by Benaud in the first over, and the 4 wickets which Australia
had striven for in vain the previous day fell for only 16 runs.

Depeiza batted for 330 minutes and hit sixteen fours. Atkinson lasted twenty-one minutes longer than his partner and during that time scored 97 more runs, hitting altogether twenty-nine fours, one five and one six. Australia did not enforce the follow-on; the rest of the match was academic and a draw.

The fifth and final Test was one of the most extraordinary ever played. The West Indies scored 357 and 319, figures good enough to win more Test Matches than they will lose. Yet they lost this one by an innings and 82 runs. It was a match of many records. First and foremost was the performance by Walcott in hitting for the second time during the series two separate centuries in a match, a feat never before accomplished. Furthermore, he became the first player to reach three figures on five occasions in a Test rubber. The Australian total of 758 for 8 declared, besides being the biggest ever recorded in a Test Match by a side from the Commonwealth, yielded two other records, the scoring of five centuries in an innings, and the highest stand for the third wicket in history for Australia. Statistics will suffice to tell the story of the match. For the West Indies: Walcott 155 and 110; Sobers 35 not out and 64; Weekes 56; Worrell 61. Australia: McDonald 127; Harvey 204; Miller 109; Archer 128; Benaud 121. Of the bowlers the least said the soonest mended, except for Miller, who took 6 for 107 in the West Indies first innings. So ended the series, convincingly for Australia – three to nothing and two drawn.

In January 1956 the West Indies made their first full-scale tour of New Zealand. They won the Test series by three games to one, but it is problematical whether victor or vanquished had more reason for satisfaction at the outcome. With the sole aim of preparing young players for sterner tests ahead, the West Indies included only three professionals in Atkinson's team. Ramadhin and Valentine provided experience in attack, and from the batting trio of Weekes, Worrell and Walcott, they chose Weekes. How very heavily the side leaned on these three, and on Atkinson, can be seen from the averages: Weekes achieved a Test average of 83·60 and Atkinson 36, while the next best average was 22·33 by H. Furlonge. Atkinson headed the bowling, with Ramadhin second and Valentine fourth. Collie Smith came third with 13 wickets at an average of 18·53. The disappointing form of the young batsmen placed an enormous burden on the broad shoulders of Weekes, but he bore the mantle magnificently, hitting six centuries in his ten first-class innings. In each of his first five innings he made a century, two of them in Tests, and he followed with another in the third Test.

For their part, New Zealand, who, when this series began had played forty-one Tests without winning one, at long last captured that elusive victory in the fourth Test. Local offices closed and excited crowds streamed to the Eden Park ground on the last afternoon as Cave and Beard routed the West Indies for their lowest score in Test Cricket – 77. The West Indies had begun the Test series by bowling New Zealand out for 74, Ramadhin taking 6 for 23. With 123 from Weekes, the West Indies scored 353, and bowled New Zealand out a second time for 208. Weekes scored 103 in the second Test, in which the West Indies made 386 and bowled New Zealand out twice to win by an innings and 64 runs. It was Ramadhin and Valentine again who did most of the damage, with a valuable contribution from a third spinning partner, Collie Smith, who took 6 wickets in the two innings. The West Indies won the third Test by 9 wickets, all revolving round Weekes again and his third test century (156), and then to Auckland, where Dewdney, in the first innings, and Atkinson, in the second, bowled well enough to have won any Test Match: Dewdney took 5 for 21 and Atkinson 7 for 53. New Zealand's scores of 255 and 157 for 9 declared hardly looked good enough to win a Test Match against the West Indies, but Weekes failed, and they virtually all failed except Furlonge, who batted defiantly for 64 in the first innings. At one time in their second innings the West Indies were 22 for 6 against the hostile swing bowling of Cave and Beard.

The curiosity of the tour was that S.C. Guillen, the former West Indies Test player, played for New Zealand. The touring team raised no objection, but the question was raised as to whether the rules of the Imperial Cricket Conference had not been infringed by his inclusion. These stipulate that a player must reside in his adopted country for four years before representing it in Test cricket. Guillen, it was reported, had been in residence only just over three years when he won his New Zealand cap in the second Test.

In 1954–5 the West Indies did not win a match in the series – for the first time since 1939 in England. Now, two series later, in England in 1957, they failed again, losing three matches and drawing two. It was a complete anti-climax after their all-conquering tour of 1950. One reason for their failure, was that in the first place England were unquestionably a much better side, in contrast to which the West Indies, for a variety of reasons, were nothing like as effective as they had been on their earlier tour. They brought a side which was a blend of experience and youth: J.D.C. Goddard (captain), F.C.M. Alexander, N. Asgarali, D. Atkinson, T. Dewdney, A.G. Ganteaume, R. Gilchrist, W. Hall, R. Kanhai, B.H. Pairaudeau, S. Ramadhin, G. Sobers, O.G. Smith, A.L. Valentine, C.L. Walcott, E.D. Weekes and F.M. Worrell. It suffered a great deal from injury and illness, but basically, against English cricket in one of its golden periods, it was not good enough. Everton Weekes had a tragic tour in which he was plagued by sinus (the spot was punctured and drained three times without effecting a cure), Walcott pulled a muscle in the first Test, and Valentine fractured his nose – he had not hit form at the beginning of the season, and this injury affected him in the latter part. Of the quick bowlers, Gilchrist was very fast but did little with the ball; Wesley Hall, on his first trip, had all sorts of trouble with his run-up, and was never seen at his best; and Dewdney, who was a good swing bowler and very accurate, but not quick enough, the type of bowler England batsmen play so well. With Valentine's failure, and the lack of success of the quick bowlers, Ramadhin found he was almost a stock bowler, and in any event he was now a very different bowler from the one he was in 1950, because he had had to adapt himself to league cricket. In 1950 he was a killer bowler; he never gave a thought about the batsman he was bowling at. Once when he got Cyril Washbrook out in 1950 he asked what his name was as the batsman was on his way back to the pavilion! Moreover, in league matches the bowler does not have the help of world-class fielders. Ramadhin had become more conscious of field-placing and of the dangers of being hit, though he was still a fine bowler.

The failure of players of the class of Weekes and Walcott seemed to have a damaging effect on the younger batsman, except, of course, for the one shining young star – Collie Smith. (He had been christened Carl Smith, but as his closest childhood friend was also named Carl the younger Smith became 'Carly' and then 'Collie'.) His team-mates called him 'The Mighty Mouse' or 'The Wayside Preacher', because he was known also for reading lessons in church. In only his third game for Jamaica he scored 169 against the Australians; he then scored 44 and 104 in his first Test. He was a powerful hitter of the ball, once hitting six sixes and four fours in an innings of 79. In his first Test of this series he scored 161 and so scored a century in his first Test against both Australia and England. One six at Edgbaston off Jim Laker broke the tiles on the ladies' balcony over long-on. His cricket was a visible expression of his nature; it mingled skill, daring and instinct and, above all, it had joy in every step. It was one of the cruellest of tragedies when this happy young man lost his life in a motoring accident; his was an irreparable loss to cricket.

Yet this England tour which ended in failure was so near to success. England were on the floor in the first Test at Edgbaston. It looked as if 1950 was to be re-enacted all over again. Ramadhin, at his most menacing, had weaved one of his all too familiar patterns of destruction: he took 7 for 49. It looked as if the batting was roughly as before, with Walcott scoring 90 and Worrell 81, and worse still for England, a new star, Smith, had hammered 161. The rout of England continued in their second innings – 113 for 3. Defeat by an innings looked inevitable. Cowdrey now joined May; unless something could be done about Ramadhin the result of the series looked just as inevitable.

What May and Cowdrey did about Ramadhin remains as the legend of Edgbaston; nothing before, or since, has produced its equal. They added 411 for the fourth wicket – May 285 not out, Cowdrey 154. Ramadhin, in a marathon performance, bowled 774 balls, the most ever delivered by a bowler in a Test Match, beating Verity's 766 against South Africa in the time-less Test in Durban in 1939. He also bowled the most balls – 588 – in any single first-class innings. His match figures stand out in vivid contrast: 7 for 49 in the first innings, 2 for 179 in the second. When Asgarali (a substitute) caught Cowdrey at long-on the stand had prospered for eight hours and twenty minutes. May began his effort at twenty minutes to six on the Saturday evening and when he declared at twenty minutes past three on the Tuesday his heroic effort had lasted a total of five minutes short of ten hours. May, unquestionably, was England's greatest post-war batsman. The West Indies were demoralised, as any side would have been in the circumstances. In the two hours and twenty minutes of cricket that remained, they lost 7 wickets for 72. What a piece of cricket folklore it would have been if England had won!

But this was more than a drawn cricket match. It had strong psychological connotations. England believed that they had the measure of Ramadhin, and whether they had or not, believing was half the battle. On the evidence of this match, too, John Goddard must have had reservations on several counts, notably about his attack, so the teams met for the second Test at Lord's in a frame of mind diametrically opposed to the first morning at Edgbaston.

The match confirmed England's hopes; it realised the West Indies' worst fears. They were bowled out for 127 by a superb piece of controlled seam bowling by Trevor Bailey, in which he took 7 for 44. England, although 34 for 3, and looking to be wilting in the face of a hostile piece of fast bowling by Gilchrist, amassed 424. It was Cowdrey again, this time with 152. May, after the Lord Mayor's Show, was out for 0. Cricket, the fasci-nating game!

Weekes, battling gamely against adversity, hit 90 in the second innings, and Sobers, scoring his second 50 of the series, showed a portent of things to come, but the West Indies lost this match by an innings and 36 runs.

At Trent Bridge, on the feather-bed of all feather-beds, England scored 619 for 6, Graveney at his most elegant and fluent registering the highest score of his career – 258. Peter Richardson and Peter May also hit centuries. But the West Indies had their heroes too. Frank Worrell, opening with Garry Sobers, carried his bat for a superb 191. Some critics described this as the best innings he ever played. Worrell did not think so: he said modestly that on this wicket the bowler had no chance. A brilliant 168 by Collie Smith in the second innings earned West Indies a draw. The fact that Worrell had opened with Sobers underlined one of the West Indies problems. They had no Rae and Stollmeyer this time. In the first Test it had been Kanhai (42 and 1), and Pairaudeau (1 and 7); in the second Test Asgarali (0 and 26) and Kanhai (34 and 0); in the third, Worrell (191 not out and 16), Sobers (47 and 9); in the fourth, Worrell (29 and 7) and Sobers (4 and 29); and in the fifth, Worrell (4 and 0) and Asgarali (29 and 7).

But still, after three Tests, England were only one up, two were drawn, and two remained to be played. The West Indies could still win the series. The issue was settled at Leeds, decisively. England scored only 279 but it was enough to bring them an innings victory. It was all over by a quarter to three on the Saturday afternoon, the West Indies making 142 (Loader 6 for 36) and 132 (Loader 3 for 50). In the first innings the last 4 West Indies wickets were taken in four balls: Trueman bowled Collie Smith with the last ball of an over, and then Loader got a hat-trick by removing Goddard, Ramadhin and Gilchrist.

With the series now decided, the final Test at the Oval was rather more of a formality, although in order to redeem their reputation the West Indies were obviously keen to win. By a quarter past two on the Saturday it was all over. The West Indies were bowled out for 89 and 86 after England had scored 412, with centuries by Richardson and Graveney. There had been discussions on the pitch before the match began. One writer likened it in physical appearance to a slice of bread and strawberry jam. It was said in defence of the groundsman that heavy rain during the previous week had hindered preparation and much of the dressing remained on top, where it had caked. As a result, as the match progressed, the ball began to turn at very awkward angles, and Lock and Laker became as unplayable as makes no difference. Against them only Sobers enhanced his reputation.

So the tour ended in disappointment. But Sobers, Kanhai and Hall were to exact their revenge in the years to come.

Before the West Indies met England again – this time in the West Indies, where for the second successive series against England they did not win a match – they played two series against Pakistan, one in each country, and one series in India. The Pakistan contest was close; the India one decisive, for the West Indies.

When Pakistan paid their first visit to the West Indies in the early months of 1958 it brought together two immensely strong batting sides, both of which were less strong in bowling. On the plumb West Indian wickets this seemed to presage very high scoring. And that is precisely what happened. In the first Test at Bridgetown, after following on 473 runs behind, Pakistan hit their record score for a Test Match of 657 for 8 declared. Hanif Mohammad – 'The Little Master' – set up a new record for the longest innings in first-class cricket: he batted for sixteen hours and thirteen minutes for 337 – 28 runs short of beating Hutton's record of 364, but taking nearly three hours longer over it. Nevertheless, Hutton's record did not survive the tour. Garfield Sobers, then twenty-one and making his first Test century in the third Test at Kingston, hit 365 not out in ten hours and eight minutes – three hours and twelve minutes less than Hutton. Nasimul Ghani, the Pakistan left-arm slow bowler, contributed another sort of record. At 16 years 248 days, he became the youngest Test player in history. But Sobers overshadowed all the other competitors; he followed his record score with a century in each innings of the fourth Test. He totalled 824 runs in the Tests, only three short of the record for a West Indies player made by Walcott against the Australians in 1955.

The tour also saw the first Test appearance of Conrad Hunte, a magnificent player, elegant in all that he did, a batsman out of the top drawer. He signalled his class immediately by hitting a century in his first Test and played a wonderful innings of 260 before being run out in the third. Also making his début in this series was another world-class player, Lance Gibbs, a master of off-break bowling – that beautiful and difficult art, the art of a craftsman, and Gibbs indeed was that. Like the masters before him, he toiled and spun until his fingers bled; he studied the world's batsmen until he could bowl to their weaknesses in his sleep. Sometimes he had to buy his wickets, if that was the only way, but you had to watch him like a fly watching a spider or he would have you enmeshed in his web. When he had the scent of blood in his nostrils he was a beguiling sight, like a hunter closing in on his unfortunate prey.

The West Indies won the series by three matches to one and one drawn. The statistics of this prolific scoring tour were: first Test, West Indies 579 for 9 declared (Hunte 142, Weekes 197), and 28 for no wicket, Pakistan 106 (Gilchrist 4 for 32) and 657 for 8 declared (Hanif Mohammad 337) – match drawn; second Test, West Indies 325 (Kanhai 96) and 312, Pakistan 282 and 235 – West Indies won by 120 runs; third Test, Pakistan 328 (Imtiaz 122), and 288 (Wazir Mohammad 106), West Indies 790 for 3 declared (Sobers 365 not out, Hunte 260) – West Indies won by an innings and 174 runs; fourth Test, Pakistan 408 (Saeed Ahmed 150) and 318, West Indies 410 (Sobers 125, Walcott 145) and 317 for 2 (Sobers 109, Hunte 114) – West Indies won by 8 wickets; fifth Test, West Indies 268 and 227, Pakistan 496 (Wazir Mohammad 189) – Pakistan won by an innings and 1 run. The West Indians, of course, will think mainly of Hunte and Sobers at Kingston. They came together when the score was 87 for 1. When Hunte was run out (this seemed the only likely way of either of them ever getting out) the score had mounted to 533. Two Pakistan bowlers will never forget it. The 'Great' Fazal – and he was a fine bowler – took 2 for 247 and Khan Mohammad 0 for 259 – enough to drive any bowler to drink or to an early retirement! So elated were the crowd that they swarmed over the field and the pitch became so damaged that the umpires ordered repairs and no play was possible in the last hour of the fourth day. Hunte and Sobers: names to conjure with for a long time to come.

When the West Indies went to Pakistan the following winter the tables were turned. Pakistan won a three-match series, which followed the West Indies five-match Indian tour, by two games to one, the West Indies having won the Indian series, three nil, with two drawn. The Indian story introduced yet another emergence of West Indies cricket. There was no Weekes, no Worrell and no Walcott, but there were Garry Sobers, Basil Butcher, Joe Solomon and Rohan Kanhai. And there were Hall and Gilchrist to provide an awesome bowling combination – pace with fire. Alexander led the side ably, and in the Kanpur Test helped to retrieve a lost cause with the bat. Gilchrist was omitted when the team moved on to Pakistan; his absence may well have contributed to the loss of the three-match rubber. The West Indies swept through the Indian subcontinent just as they had done through the green fields of England in 1950. They overwhelmed all opposition, until losing to Pakistan on the mat at Karachi, after being put in to bat by Fazal Mahmood. Fazal converted the second Test at Dacca into a personal triumph, taking 12 for 100. Kanhai and Sobers found their masterly touch in the third Test and Pakistan were beaten for the first time in their own country.

In the first Test at Bombay in November 1958 India saved the game after struggling for most of the way. The feature of the match was the 142 not out by Sobers in the West Indies second innings. The West Indies won the second Test, Sobers again getting a big score in the second innings; this time he was run-out for 198. The third Test was a massacre: West Indies 614 for 5 declared (Kanhai 256, Butcher 103, Sobers 106 not out); India 124 and 154. This was Kanhai's first century in Test cricket – and what a beginning! He batted for six and a half hours and hit forty-two fours, an innings of dazzling conception.

The West Indies continued to pile on the runs in the fourth

Test, scoring 500 – Kanhai run out 99, Butcher 142. Kanhai just missed his second successive Test century, but Butcher achieved his. Here was another fine cricketer – Basil Butcher; bowlers of the world came to hold him in high esteem. India lost this fourth Test by 295 runs, but made a worthy score themselves in the final Test – 415 (Borde 109, Contractor 92). But still the West Indies had no difficulty in topping this. They scored 644 for 8 (Holt 123, Smith 100, Solomon 100 not out and Hunte 92). The batting had been prolific. Solomon headed the batting averages with 117·00, followed by Sobers (92·83), Butcher (69·42) and Kanhai (67·25), and the Indians seemed to have had little taste for Hall and Gilchrist who blasted their way to 56 Test wickets – Gilchrist 26, with an average of 16·11, and Hall 30, with one of 17·66.

In Pakistan it was a different story. The West Indies went down on the matting at Karachi by 10 wickets. They were put out in the first Test for 146, in which Butcher fought valiantly to make 45 not out. Fazal Mahmood took 4 wickets for 35. A century by Hanif set Pakistan on their way to a score of 304, and a second failure by most of the West Indies accredited batsmen gave Pakistan a 10-wicket victory. In a remarkably low-scoring second Test, Pakistan won by 41 runs. For Fazal Mahmood it was yet another triumph of sizeable proportions. After Pakistan seemed to have failed – they were all out for 145 – Fazal took 6 for 34. The West Indies, having been 68 for 5, lost their last 5 wickets for 8 runs, their last six batsmen – Smith, Solomon, E. Atkinson, Gibbs, Hall and Ramadhin all failing to score! They were all out for 76. Bowlers continued to dominate utterly. Hall, who had taken 4 for 28 in Pakistan's first innings, struck again and took 4 for 49 as Pakistan fell for 144. The West Indies were set to score 214 to win; they were all out for 172, Fazal taking 6 for 66 to finish with the magnificent figures, previously noted, of 12 for 100. In the third and final Test the West Indies at last hit the jackpot with another double century of scintillating stroke-play by Kanhai. They hit 469 and bowled Pakistan out for 209 and 104 to win by an innings and 156 runs. In the first innings it had been Hall; in the second Ramadhin and Gibbs. Wes Hall did the hat-trick. Mushtaq Mohammad, making his début for Pakistan at the age of 14 years and 125 days, became the youngest cricketer ever to play in a Test match.

And so to the auld enemy – England. It was an almost entirely new England side which set sail for the Caribbean on 8 December 1959. They returned four months later having accomplished something unique. By winning the second Test on the Queen's Park ground in Trinidad, and drawing the other four games, they won a series in the West Indies for the first time in history. Sadly, the second lingering memory of this tour was the riot which disfigured the second Test in Trinidad, a scene of shame and disgrace so deeply deplored by all Trinidadians, sportsmen, administrators, not to mention those entirely unconnected with sport but with a strong sense of pride in their island. Happily, it did not stain the good relations between the two teams; it was a horrible outburst by rum-filled hooligans which could have had unthinkable consequences. It was bad enough as it was. For England, the silver lining was victory – the only one of the series. The main reason for the lack of positive results were the pitches, which were made to last six days and rarely produced even a modicum of turn on the last day. In the main it was a paradise for batsmen. The two captains were both former Cambridge blues – Gerry Alexander and Peter May. The latter, however, was compelled to return home because of an illness which necessitated an operation, and Cowdrey, an Oxford blue, took over the captaincy. Subba Row, a Cambridge blue, became vice-captain of the English team. It was Alexander and May who tossed up at Bridgetown. May won and England batted. The West Indies side in batting order was: Hunte, McMorris, Kanhai, Sobers, Worrell, Butcher, Hall, Alexander, Scarlett, Watson and Ramadhin. Of these England had not seen McMorris, the opener, Butcher, who was already making plenty of runs, Scarlett, an off-spinner, and Watson, a fast bowler. Two Barbadians, Nurse and Griffith, were not included, to the chagrin of the Bajans.

England took full advantage of the toss and the wicket. They scored 482, Barrington making 128 and Dexter 136 not out.

The 1928 team – the first to play an official Test Match.
Standing: J.E. Scheult, W.St Hill, E.A. Rae, E.L.G. Hoad, J.A. Small,
F.R. Martin, L.N. Constantine, J. Neblett, O.C. Scott.
Seated: E.L. Bartlett, M.P. Fernandes,
C.V. Wight, R.K. Nunes (Captain), G. Challenor, C.R. Browne.

The great 1950 team to England.
Standing: C.B. Williams, R.E. Marshall, A.L. Valentine, L.R. Pierre, C.L. Walcott,
H.H. Johnson, A.F. Rae, K. Trestrail, W. Ferguson (scorer).
Seated: S. Ramadhin, P.E. Jones, F.M. Worrell, Rev. Palmer Barnes (assistant manager),
J.D. Goddard (Captain), G.E. Gomez, J.B. Stollmeyer, R.J. Christiani, E.D. Weekes.

G. Challenor, the 'father figure' of West Indian batsmanship.

I. Barrow, wicket-keeper batsman of the highest class.

E.R. Martindale, fast bowler of exceptional pace and ability.

C.A. Roach, scorer of the first centur and first double century in Test cricke

George Headley.

Everton Weekes.

'Sonny' Ramadhin.

Alfred Valentine.

'Wes' Hall.

Clyde Walcott.

Garry Sobers.

Clive Lloyd.

Lord 'Learie' Constantine and Sir Frank Worrell.

Clyde Walcott steers one past Cowdrey in the slips
in the first Test at Edgbaston, 1957.

December, 1960: the tied Test at Brisbane.
Meckiff is dramatically run out and history is made.

Lord's, 1963: Derek Shackleton is run out by Frank Worrell as 'Wes' Hall appeals.
This brought Colin Cowdrey to the wicket with his broken arm in plaster,
and two balls to go. David Allen faced them both successfully.

Lance Gibbs.   Charlie Griffith.

Rohan Kanhai.   Conrad Hunte.

The presentation of the Prudential Cup Trophy at Lord's, 1975. Clive Lloyd, who hit a brilliant 102, received the trophy from the Duke of Edinburgh after the West Indies' victory over Australia by 17 runs.

The Prudential Cup Winning Squad 1975.
Standing: C.G. Greenidge, M.L.C. Foster, I.V.A. Richards, K.D. Boyce, V.A. Holder, A.M.E. Roberts, C. King, B.D. Julien, A.I. Kallicharran. *Seated:* R.B. Kanhai, D.L. Murray, C.H. Lloyd (Captain), C.L. Walcott (Manager), L.R. Gibbs, R.C. Fredericks

The West Indies did even better, owing to a partnership of huge proportions by Sobers and Worrell. They took the score from 102 for 3 to 501 for 4, Sobers scoring 226 and Worrell 197 not out, only the declaration at 563 for 8 preventing Worrell from reaching his double century. England were without Statham, who had damaged a hamstring muscle by a fall in the game against Barbados. England missed him greatly. Sobers batted for ten hours, forty-seven minutes, and Worrell for eleven hours and twenty minutes, which were the two longest innings ever played against England. When the declaration came, the West Indies were 81 ahead with only two hours and forty minutes of the match remaining, and twenty minutes of this was lopped off by rain. England were 71 without loss when this match of 18 wickets and 1,116 runs moved quietly to its end. Alexander established a new West Indies wicket-keeping record by dismissing five batsmen in an innings.

And so to Trinidad, where again May won the toss, again England batted first, and again there were two century-makers – Barrington, for the second time, and M.J.K. Smith. The England total reached 382 and there seemed no reason why West Indies should not follow suit. They were 22 for no wicket at the end of the second day. However, the third day proved to be full of unpredictable events and of macabre twists and turns. Statham and Trueman broke through immediately and decisively: the West Indies were 45 for 5 and suddenly the innings was in pieces. It was saved from total destruction by Alexander and Ramadhin. Alexander batted with grim determination for over two hours for 28. Four runs later, Ramadhin called Singh for a sharp single to cover; Dexter hurled the ball in to the top of the stumps and Singh was run out. Hardly had Lee Kow's finger gone up when a storm of booing was followed by a torrent of bottles, thrown like hand-grenades, from all corners of the ground. May called his boundary fielders in, and in no time only a tiny island round the wicket itself was free of bottles. Alexander rushed out and talked with May, and, flanked by police officers, the players left the field. On the field all hell was let loose: mobs were fighting; the police, pathetically few, could do nothing; bottles, many of them broken before-

D

hand, rained a cascade of terror. Trinidad officials, including
Learie Constantine, went out into the thick of it. They were
helpless until, three-quarters of an hour after the first bottle had
been thrown, mounted police with tin-hatted reinforcements
appeared on the scene. The rioters scattered, the brawlers dis-
persed. There were thirty hospital cases and another sixty
received running repairs on the spot. The Premier, Dr Eric
Williams, sent the following telegram:

President MCC, Lord's, London, England
On behalf of the Government and people of Trinidad and Tobago
I send my deepest regrets and apologies for incidents which caused
disruption of the second Test Match here today in Port of Spain.
I am happy to inform you that there has not been the slightest
hostility directed against the MCC as a team or any individual
player. We shall do our best to ensure that the happy connections
on the fields of cricket and other fields of sport which have always
existed between us and you will not in any way be prejudiced by this
occurrence.
Learie Constantine, my Minister of Works and Transport, asks to
be personally associated with this message. He and I have already
expressed our personal apologies to Mr Peter May, Captain of the
MCC, and Mr R.W.V. Robins, Manager, and I am most glad to
say that our regrets and apologies were most graciously received.

After the long weekend it was back to cricket. There was
absolutely no truth whatsoever in rumours that England might
not continue the match; the question never arose, and Robins
himself had swiftly scotched this fantasy. The West Indies were
finally out for 112. May surprised some (but by no means
everyone) by batting again, even though he had a lead of 270.
With a further 230 for 9 he increased this to 500, and, despite
110 by Kanhai, the West Indies could manage only 244, and so
lost by 256 runs.

What England had, they held for the next three drawn Test
Matches, matches memorable for the almost wholly sustained
brilliance of Sobers. He had made 226 in Barbados, 0 and 31 in
Trinidad, followed by 147 and 19 at Kingston, 145 at Georgetown and 92 and 49 not out in the second match in Trinidad. In
the series, he scored 709 runs at an average of over 101, beating

George Headley's 703 in 1929–30, previously the highest for the
West Indies against England. The other batsmen did not support
Sobers as might have been expected of them. Worrell and
Kanhai played one big innings each, and Hunte was consistent,
though his top score was 72, and in an effort to increase the
scoring-rate, the West Indies selectors recalled Walcott from
Test retirement. Walcott made a 50 in the final Test, but the
move was not really the success that had been hoped for.
Ramadhin headed the bowling averages, but Wes Hall,
showing amazing stamina which enabled him to sustain his pace
for over after over – and he was bowling really fast – took the
most wickets. Watson gave him reasonable support; but none
could match the great bowling of Trueman. 'Fiery Fred' he
was aptly called – perhaps a little too much fire, but magnificent
bowling all the same.

The Third Test in Jamaica was crucial for the West Indies.
Cowdrey made it safe for England with 114 in the first innings
and 97 in the second. The century by Sobers was supported by
McMorris, who hit 73, and a new name to English supporters –
Seymour Nurse. We were to hear much more of him. The
scores in this third Test were: England 277 and 305, West
Indies 353 and 175 for 6. Wes Hall's bowling in England's
first innings – 7 for 69 – easily surpassed any other bowling
performance of the match.

The West Indies were looking, both in Georgetown in the
fourth Test, and in Trinidad in the fifth, to win the toss. They
failed in all five Tests. Some will say this was the only difference
between the sides, others that things would not have been very
different whichever side had won the toss, although five out of
five is certainly monopolising the luck. At Georgetown, however, England's first innings score of 295 was nothing to write
home about, and it put the West Indies in the game with a
chance. They scored 402 for 8 (Sobers 145) and were hoping to
be able to prise England out a second time, but centuries by
Subba Row and Dexter, and a score of 334 for 8, meant that the
West Indies would have to throw in their heavy artillery for the
final match of the series in Port of Spain, the scene of bitter, yet
happy, memories for England.

At one time on the fifth day of the fifth Test the West Indies seemed to have created a wonderful chance for themselves: England were 148 for 6 in their second innings. In their first innings England had scored 393, and the West Indies 338 for 8 declared, which meant that the visitors had a lead of 55. At 148 for 6, England were 203 on and precariously poised. But at this moment a tactical ploy paid handsome dividends. England had included Jim Parks as wicket-keeper instead of Swetman in an effort to strengthen their batting. He joined Mike Smith and the two took the score from 148 for 6 to 345 for 7 – Parks 101 not out and Smith 96. England were safe. Cowdrey was determined to keep them that way, and his declaration was delayed until not even one of cricket's miracles could win the game for the West Indies. They were set to score 406 to win at 140 an hour. When catching Smith to break the decisive stand, Alexander equalled the world's wicket-keeping record of 23 dismissals in a series – and he was on the losing side.

5   Swinging Sixties

Never has it been more apparent that the game is greater than the result than in Melbourne on February 17, 1961. Commerce in this Australian city stood almost still as the smiling cricketers from the West Indies, the vanquished not the victors, were given a send-off the like of which is normally reserved for Royalty and national heroes. Open cars paraded the happy players from the Caribbean among hundreds and thousands of Australians who had been sentimentalised through the media [*sic*] of cricket as it should be played. Worrell, the handsome West Indies captain, Hall, a bowler big in heart as well as stature, Kanhai, a fleet-footed batsman in the best tradition, and the suave Ramadhin, who had come a long way since he was introduced to cricket at the Canadian Mission School in Trinidad, were among those, whom it was said, were moved to tears by the enthusiasm of the farewell.

Thus did *Wisden* report on the West Indies in Australia in 1960–1. For the most part, the sixties were golden days for West Indies cricket. Before falling to Australia in 1968–9 and England in 1969, at the tail-end of the decade, the West Indies had played thirty-three Tests between 1960–1 and 1967–8 and lost only six of them. They punished India by seven matches to nothing, beat England three to one, twice, and beat Australia for the first time in a series, two to one, in 1964–5, and of course they had begun this period in their history by participating in the first tied Test Match in cricket's long life. These were wonderful days and it must never be forgotten anywhere in the Caribbean just how much was owed to the magnetic leadership of Frank Worrell. His team would have followed him over the edge of a cliff if necessary; and his opponents had respect and great affection for him. In retrospect, probably the sixties were some of the happiest years for world cricket, years in which the

West Indies played a principal role. Some of us can see now in
our mind's eye Frank Worrell during a long innings, a regal
majesty surrounding him, as the sun climbed up into the sky
and paused in the noon heat before descending towards
evening, while the field turned a softer and softer green, the
changing day being a reflection of his cricket – all sun and
shadow, and inevitability.

It may seem incongruous in the present mood of the seventies
with its obsessional focus on winning, to say that, although the
West Indies lost the 1960–1 series in Australia by two matches
to one with one tied, the losing mattered not at all. But it
happens to be true. Cricket was the overall winner of this series,
and the game does not win every series – not by a long chalk.
It takes two to make a cricket match, and Frank Worrell was
perhaps fortunate that Australia had a great captain, too, in
Richie Benaud. And what a way to start a series – with a tie!
Brisbane had never seen the likes of it before, and surely never
will again.

Every indication, at the end of the two first innings – West
Indies 453, and Australia 505 – was that these massive scores
could only lead to a drawn game. Sobers, with 132, and a huge
innings for Australia of 181 by Norman O'Neill, had been
fairly consistently supported by other players, and the wicket
looked as good as could be. The West Indies, however, did not
fare as well in the second innings, and Australia were set to
score 233 at a rate of 45 runs an hour for victory. But they were
ravaged by Hall, who broke the first part of the Australian
innings to pieces with a fiery piece of fast bowling of the highest
quality. Australia were 57 for 5 and tottering. Could Hall
maintain this blistering pace much longer? Mackay was out
at 92 and this brought Davidson and Benaud together in what
was absolutely a last-ditch effort. Now the game began to build
up into the dramatic crescendo of its pulsating last few minutes.
Davidson, who had had a superb match (11 wickets and 44
runs in the first innings), dominated what looked like a life-
saving partnership. Benaud dropped anchor with him and
with a rugged piece of fighting cricket Australia moved slowly
into a position where defeat was behind them and victory

looked just round the corner. The score had mounted to 226 for 6 and they were weathering the new ball which Hall had taken half an hour before time, with 27 runs needed for victory. This was the West Indies last throw of the dice and it brought Hall's last supreme effort, this time against bookmakers' odds.

The partnership was broken when Benaud called Davidson for a sharp single and Joe Solomon hit the stumps from mid-wicket to run Davidson out. Grout came in, and took a single off Sobers, so that when the last momentous eight-ball over from Hall began, Australia needed 6 runs for victory with 3 wickets still standing. This was to be the most melodramatic over ever bowled, an over that raised blood-pressures beyond surgical limits! If a whole book were ever to be written about one over alone, then this is the one.

Grout faced the first ball and was hit a painful blow on the thigh. Benaud, giving him no chance to work out whether he wanted a doctor or an undertaker, called Grout for a sharp single, Benaud desperately wanting the strike himself. Grout hobbled home. Hall's next ball to Benaud was a rearing bumper, more than head-high, and Benaud's flailing hook managed only a flick from the gloves to the keeper and he was caught. This left Meckiff, Kline and Grout to face six balls with 5 runs to make. Meckiff blocked the first ball, swung at the next down the leg-side, missed, and as he was contemplating what he might have done had he connected, he suddenly found that Grout was bearing down on him looking for the strike. Alexander threw the ball to Hall, Hall flung it at the stumps at the bowler's end, and it would have gone for four overthrows but for Alfred Valentine's despairing dive. So both sides breathed again. Four runs to get, four balls to be bowled. Nervous tension gripped everybody, players and spectators alike, and became all the more evident from the next bizarre interlude. Grout, forcing on the on-side, spooned the ball just behind square-leg. Kanhai stood there, perfectly positioned for the catch. Somehow, and few people know just how, Wes Hall, keyed up to the limit of human endurance, arrived at the spot just as Kanhai was taking the catch, and in the inevitable collision the ball dropped to the ground. If this had not

occurred at an absolute crisis point in a Test Match, it would
have provided a good laugh all round; the sort that brings the
house down at a circus. The result was a single to Australia.
Hall, recovering from the travesty, pitched the next ball
perfectly. Meckiff, a 6-handicap golfer, played a good golf shot
and lofted the ball away almost into the mid-wicket fence. It
stopped in some high clover. Meckiff and Grout crossed for
one, for two, and the scores were level as Hunte picked up the
ball from 80 yards away and with a magnificent throw sent it
on its way back to Alexander. As it flashed through the air,
Meckiff and Grout had crossed for the winning run, but Grout
never quite made it to the wicket-keeper's end. As it was,
covered in grass and dust, he trudged back, despair and misery
written all over his face; en route he passed Lindsay Kline,
looking as if he was on his way to the gallows instead of to a
game of cricket!

Kline's brief was clear. He had to make 1 run for Australia
to win a Test Match. Up came Hall, pounding in. It was make
or break; the off-side fieldsmen moved in as he gathered
momentum; a run here would be hard to find. On the leg-side,
Joe Solomon was just in front of square-leg, his cap on, and his
left hand shielding his eyes from the setting sun. For a number
11, Kline played the ball with some skill, wide of Solomon.
Worrell rushed for the bowler's end to take the throw; Solomon,
as cool as an ice-pack, promptly threw the wicket down at the
wicket-keeper's end where no one was backing up. Australia
could have won the match twice on overthrows; they could
have won it with the Kanhai–Hall dropped catch; instead, this
marvellous game of cricket ended in a tie.

When it was all over Wes Hall started the calypsos after
demolishing a few beers, a gigantic pawpaw, and a couple of
mangoes sent in by well-wishers. Cammie Smith and Seymour
Nurse provided some sound à-la-steel band; they were inspired,
possibly, by the earlier sight of Gerry Gomez and Norman
O'Neill doing what served for an Irish jig on the little lawn in
front of the players' dressing-room. It was all rather like *Alice
in Wonderland* and the Mad Hatter – and had Alice and the
Mad Hatter been playing they could hardly have provided

more bizarre entertainment than that last over. Posterity will always want to know the names of the participants, to be stored away in cricket's treasure-chest. Here they are:

AUSTRALIA: McDonald, Simpson, Harvey, O'Neill, Favell, Mackay, Davidson, Benaud (captain), Grout, Meckiff, Kline. WEST INDIES: Hunte, Cammie Smith, Kanhai, Sobers, Worrell (captain), Solomon, Lashley, Alexander, Ramadhin, Hall, Valentine.

And this was only the first Test; there were four more to come!

The second Test at Melbourne produced some extraordinary batting failures for the West Indies. After Australia had scored 348, Nurse hit 70 and Kanhai 84. The scores of the other nine players were: 1, 0, 9, 0, 5, 0, 5, 4, 1. This meant that two batsmen between them scored 154, out of the West Indies total of 181. The second innings was something of a replica of the first. Hunte scored 110, Kanhai 25 and Alexander 72. The other scores were: 4, 3, 0, 0, 3, 4, 5, 0. The total was 233, and Australia knocked off the 67 runs required for the loss of 3 wickets to win by 7 wickets. The high drama of Brisbane was totally lacking at Melbourne. The West Indies had disappointed and if they lost at Sydney would lose the chance of winning the series.

But at Sydney they turned the tables. They spun their way to success with the off-spin of Lance Gibbs and the left-arm bowling of Alfred Valentine. Sobers had bolstered the batting in the first innings almost single-handedly. He scored 168 out of a total of 339. Gibbs was making his first appearance in Australia and he spun himself to immediate fame by taking 3 for 46 and 5 for 66. At the other end of the spinning-wheel, Valentine took 4 for 67 and 4 for 86. After Australia had been dismissed for 202, Gerry Alexander hit his maiden Test century for the West Indies. It left Australia with the unlikely proposition of scoring 464 to win, of which they could manage only 241.

So the series had come alive again, one each and one tied,

and that is how it stayed after the fourth Test which was drawn, but which was memorable for Kanhai hitting a century in each innings, 117 and 115, and Gibbs taking a hat-trick and picking up five more wickets as well. The West Indies scored 393 and 432 for 6 declared; Australia 366 and 273 for 9. A drawn game, yes, but very nearly matching Brisbane for excitement. The West Indies, by all reasonable assumption, had won the game hands down. The situation was all but hopeless when Kline joined Mackay; an hour and fifty minutes remained, the West Indies total was far beyond reach, and the possibility of survival was remote, even taking the most optimistic view. But Mackay and Kline did survive, and saved the match. Gibb's hat-trick, incidentally, was the first against Australia this century.

Australia and the West Indies were certainly proving between them that they had all the ingredients to produce heroic cricket matches. They had stirred the imagination of the world, not just in Australia and the Caribbean, and enormous attention was focused on the last Test at Melbourne. Once again it lacked nothing in spectacular entertainment. For West Indies there was disappointment at losing, and a genuine belief that the fates were against them in one particular instance at a critical stage in the proceedings. Australia, needing 258 to win, were 254 for 7. Grout late-cut Valentine and the off-bail fell to the ground. Alexander did not turn to follow the ball's path but pointed to the broken wicket. The batsmen went through for 2, after which the umpire at the bowler's end went over to consult the square-leg umpire. The 2 runs were allowed to stand; what moved the bail can only remain conjecture. But it meant that Australia got the runs and won the series – one of the greatest Test series ever played.

When India arrived in the Caribbean the following winter they were facing a side on the crest of a wave and were completely swept off their feet. The West Indies won all five Test matches by overwhelming margins – 10 wickets, an innings and 18 runs, an innings and 30 runs, 7 wickets, and 123 runs. There was no violent swinging of the pendulum such as had characterised the series in Australia; it was all one way. The West Indies batsmen scored prolifically except Hunte, who had a rather lean time. Worrell averaged 88, Kanhai 70, Sobers 70 and McMorris 58. Hall, Gibbs and Sobers took 74 Test wickets between them, and King, making his début in the last Test, took 7 wickets for 64 – a fine start. Gibbs looked a world-beater and Sobers displayed his wide versatility as a purveyor of the 'chinaman' and the left-hander's googly.

The tour was marred by a serious injury to Contractor when he was struck by a ball from Griffith in the game against Barbados. He was rushed to hospital with a fractured skull and immediately underwent an emergency brain operation which undoubtedly saved his life. Three of his colleagues, Borde, Nadkarni and Umrigar, and the West Indies captain, Frank Worrell, gave blood. A specialist brain surgeon was flown from Trinidad and another operation followed. Mercifully, Contractor's life was saved. The scores in the Test Matches were: first Test, India 203 and 98, West Indies 289 and 15 for no wicket; second Test, India 395 and 218, West Indies 631 for 8 declared (McMorris 125, Kanhai 138, Sobers 153); third Test, India 258 and 187, West Indies 475; fourth Test, West Indies 444 for 9 declared (Kanhai 139) and 176 for 3, India 197 (Hall 5 for 20) and 422 (Umrigar 172 not out, Durrani 104); fifth Test, West Indies 253 (Sobers 104) and 283, India 178 (King 5 for 46) and 235 (Sobers 5 for 63). For West Indies it was a peak; for India, the nadir.

It was in this frame of mind that the West Indies came to England in 1963, six years after their thoroughly disappointing tour in 1957. They felt they had the resources this time to do a much better job. They were right in their estimation, winning the series by three games to one with one drawn. Of the five Cricketers of the Year chosen by *Wisden*, four were 1963 West Indian tourists: Charlie Griffith, Conrad Hunte, Rohan Kanhai and Garry Sobers. It was an appropriate tribute to a fine side. Unlike most other previous sides from the West Indies,

the majority of the 1963 team had already gained experience
of English conditions. Nine of them had held league engagements, and five had been in the 1957 team. Both wicket-
keepers, David Allan and Deryck Murray, were newcomers;
and Murray, straight from school, met Wes Hall for the first
time when the players assembled in London. Whereas, in 1950,
the one weakness in the side was fast bowling, this time it was
the inability to find a successful opening partner to Conrad
Hunte, who enjoyed a magnificent tour. As vice-captain to
Frank Worrell, Hunte had an important role to play. In a radio
broadcast at the beginning of the tour when deputising for his
captain, Hunte said: 'Our aim is to go all out to win and enjoy
ourselves doing so.' He had decided that with such an array of
stroke-makers – Kanhai, Sobers, Butcher, Nurse and Worrell –
the team needed someone to keep one end solid and secure so as
to give the team stability to match its flamboyancy. The part
fitted Hunte like a glove. He topped the Test batting averages
with 58·87, and his 182 in the first Test at Old Trafford was
the highest of the series. Hunte had reason to believe after this
performance that he was the natural successor as captain on
Frank Worrell's retirement at the end of the tour; his disappointment on being passed over in favour of Garry Sobers
was acute.

This time, the West Indies lacked nothing in their fast-
bowling armoury. Charlie Griffith, fast and fearsome, blazed
his way to 32 Test wickets at an average of 16·21. His yorker
was a sinister ball; few fast bowlers in our time have bowled a
better one. Wes Hall was a wonderful partner at the other end,
and probably the outstanding memory of the tour was the way
Frank Worrell kept Hall going in the epic Lord's Test; it was
just like a champion jockey picking up a beaten horse and
driving him past the winning-post when every ounce of strength
seemed to have drained away even before the last furlong. This
showed great leadership, and great loyalty to a leader too.
Sobers collected his share of Test wickets, and Lance Gibbs
bowled superbly. Gibbs was the supreme craftsman in an
absorbing craft, twisting his fingers over after over, racking his
brains, sometimes tossing the ball up temptingly. The West

Indies won the first Test at Old Trafford – their first Test
victory on this famous ground – and a resounding one. It was
all over at half past three on the Monday afternoon; a victory
by 10 wickets. Conrad Hunte, the architect of that victory, was
playing the role he had fashioned for himself – he scored 182
out of 398 in eight hours, twenty minutes. It was the highest
score made by a visiting player in a Test Match at Old Trafford.
The West Indies declared at 501 for 6 and then bowled England
out for 205 and 296, which left them with a mere token run to
win. Hunte scored it off the first ball from Allen, and this
brought the West Indies six successive Test wins for the first
time in their history. The master bowler was Lance Gibbs; he
took 11 wickets in the match.

And so to Lord's and a cricket match of unparalleled
emotions, thoroughly irregular heart-beats, great performances,
great courage, the twisting wheel of fortune finally spinning to a
just conclusion – a draw, a victory for both sides. It would have
been fate at its most cruel if either side had come away the
loser.

When the final over was about to be bowled, any one of four
results was possible – a win for either side, a tie or a draw – and
as if the match were a staged performance, a prearranged
melodrama in the Metro-Goldwyn-Meyer tradition worked
out by an over-zealous scriptwriter, Cowdrey appeared
through a sea of faces in the pavilion to do battle with a broken
arm in plaster. England's walking wounded were being pulled
up into the front line from the field hospitals because England
needed every man to do his duty. Cowdrey tells the story in his
own words:

There were two balls to go when I reached the crease, five runs to
win; David Allen had the strike. We conferred and David said; 'I
have not given up hope of winning; if I have the luck to get a four
off the first ball we'll scamper the last run.' Alas, Wes Hall who had
bowled nearly all day, and much of the day before, roared up and
bowled two very good deliveries, straight, and on a good length.
David did well to keep them out and save us from going two down in
the series. Just before he bowled the last ball, amid deafening noise
from an excited crowd I could hear Frank Worrell shout at the

top of his voice – 'Whatever you do don't bowl a no-ball.' 'What', shouted Wes. Worrell repeated it twice but I don't think Wes ever did hear, the adrenalin was running so fast all round. As both teams slumped into their chairs in the dressing-room it needed a little while and a long drink for us to recover from it all.

A dramatic enough finish, but then the game had begun with high drama when Hunte hit the first three balls of the match from Trueman for four. With consistent batting (Hunte 44, Kanhai 73, Solomon 56) the West Indies totalled 301. But even the first innings was neck and neck. Dexter played one of his great innings; the faster Hall and Griffith bowled, the harder he whacked them. He made 70, Barrington scored 80, and life-saving efforts by Parks and Titmus, 35 and 52 not out, took the England score to 297, within four runs of the West Indies. In the West Indies second innings Basil Butcher played what many of the best judges consider to be the finest innings of his career. He got some support from Kanhai and Worrell, but he virtually held the innings together by his own efforts. It was a fighting innings with classical connotations; some of his strokes were the true music of cricket, others were made out of sheer dogged determination to preserve his wicket. He scored 133 out of 299, which left England with 234 to win.

England's second innings produced another blood-and-guts effort by Barrington, who made 60, and an extraordinary performance by Close, who scored 70, and, with unbelievable bravado, allowed the two fast bowlers to hit him rather than play a shot and get out. At times, as if this was cricket on a heath, he would walk down the wicket to meet Wes Hall as he was pounding up on his run, and in doing so certainly succeeded once or twice in unsettling him completely. Cowdrey had disappeared from the battle when struck a crushing blow on the wrist from a ball by Wes Hall which broke it; he came back to play out the final scene.

As a result of this match, England were still alive – one down, and three to play – and in view of the parity of the two sides at Lord's, it looked like a pretty open contest. Trueman had had a fine match at Lord's, taking 11 for 152. Now, at Edgbaston, he did even better, finishing with 12 for 119, the best Test average of his whole career and a yeoman effort for a pace bowler thirty-two years old. His 7 for 44 shot the West Indies out in the second innings for 91, plunging them to defeat by 217 runs. Rain played a predominant part in the proceedings, Monday being the first day to yield unbroken cricket. England scored 216 and 278 for 9 declared, the West Indies 186 and 91. Trueman's final onslaught brought him the last 6 wickets in 24 balls, during which the only scoring stroke was a late-cut for four by Gibbs, the last man in.

Now it was level pegging, with two matches to go and England the accepted favourites. Leeds, however, belonged to Charlie Griffith, and it is interesting in retrospect to read what he wrote after the West Indies had been beaten by Yorkshire before the first Test: 'During the game I learnt a lot watching Freddie Trueman. He bowled a full length and moved the ball off the seam both ways, but what especially struck me about Freddie was the way in which he used the crease and how he controlled his speed. He used to come in close to the stumps to bowl the outswinger and he had these subtle variations of pace that troubled all of us.' Well, Charlie showed what he had learned from him on Fred's own ground at Headingley. The West Indies had got away to a good start with a century by Sobers and 92 by Kanhai. England struggled against the two extremes – pace and spin, mainly pace. Griffith took 6 for 36 and Gibbs 3 for 50. With Butcher and Sobers as the principal run-makers in the second innings, the West Indies totalled 229 (their second innings score at Lord's). Then Gibbs and Griffith, with the aid of Sobers, did it again. England were all out for 231, the West Indies had won by 221 runs and were winning two-one, with England having no chance of saving the series at the Oval. The West Indies match-winner this time was the same player as in the first Test at Old Trafford, Conrad Hunte, who scored 80 and 108 not out; although Griffith, once again, was very much on target with 9 for 137. England made 275 and 223, the West Indies 246 and 255 for 2. It was a convincing win, there was no denying it.

The final scenes were amazing. Early in the day the gates had been closed with 25,350 inside. At the end it seemed as if all 25,350 were swarming on the field like an invasion force; and the escaping players were engulfed in a sea of humanity. Thus ended an era on the crest of a wave, the era of Frank Worrell, the captain; his contribution in that role to West Indies cricket had been immeasurable. The West Indies were thus the first winners of the Wisden trophy, inaugurated to commemorate the one hundredth consecutive appearance of the famous almanack.

The visit by Australia to the West Indies in the winter of 1964–5 was billed by the cricket writers as 'The World Championship'. If it was so, then by the end of the tour the West Indians were indeed World Champions. They beat Australia, to win their first series against them by two matches to one and two drawn. After three Tests, the West Indies led two-nil, with one drawn; but here the Australians, with their traditional ability to fight back in adversity, stemmed the tide of defeat, drew the fourth Test, and won the last. As had been the case in England, controversy raged over the bowling action of Charlie Griffith; he was not no-balled, and nor had he been by the English umpires.

The West Indies owed much to five batsmen – Hunte, Kanhai, Butcher, Sobers and Nurse – but they owed even more to two individual bowling performances, Wes Hall in Jamaica, and Lance Gibbs in Guiana. Hall took 9 wickets in the first Test, and Gibbs took 9 in the third, the two Tests won by the West Indies. These two pieces of bowling were undoubtedly the decisive factors in the home team's success. This was the first series in which the West Indies were led by Sobers; it was a happy augury. Statistically, his own figures did not measure up to his composite value to the side. Surprisingly, his highest score in a Test Match was 69, yet his extraordinary consistency still produced a batting average of 39·11. His scores in the five Tests were: 30, 27, 69, 24, 45, 42, 55, 34 not out, 18 and 8. His 12 Test wickets cost him 41 runs apiece. Concealed in these figures, however, are the new captain's many virtues, his all-round talents, his very presence, which bound this team together and there is no better way of leading than by personal example.

Seymour Nurse played the supreme innings of the tour in Barbados, after Lawry and Simpson had both scored double centuries and the first Australian wicket had not fallen until 382 runs were on the board. Then Cowper, at number 3, hit a century, the second Australian wicket falling at 522. This was enough to demoralise any team, but not the West Indies. They drew the match and thus won the series, the result of the fifth Test being purely academic. Richie Benaud wrote:

It is true that Griffith occupied a lot of headlines on the tour, particularly early in the series, but fortunately the West Indies were good enough, I believe, to win without him, though he often took a vital wicket in the Test matches. The West Indies batting was superior to that of the Australians and, of course, they had the speed that the Australians lacked. The last word should be for Gary Sobers who handled his team well in his first series as captain though, as Simpson found out, it is much easier to be a winning captain than a loser. To Sobers and his team go warmest con-gratulations. The world crown of cricket rests lightly on their heads.

Though a Barbadian, Sobers must have been very happy to make his début as captain in Jamaica. It was on this ground that he made his world-record Test score of 365; he had played his first Test Match on Jamaican soil, and he had a Test batting average of over 100 on the ground. He needed only three more Tests to equal the 51 played by Frank Worrell, and provided he kept free of injury, would be able to set up a new record on this tour.

Sobers started well by winning the toss on a beautiful batting wicket. But the West Indies failed utterly to take advantage of it. They were 149 for 6, when White, a bespectacled Barbadian, playing in his first Test Match, came in and showed the way to his fallen colleagues. He took the bull by the horns and by unorthodoxy and orthodoxy, but mainly by good hard clouts, he reached 50 in forty-six minutes. Fortune favours the brave and, though he was given a life by Cowper, he revived the West Indies innings and helped push along their score, which finally reached 239. This still looked nothing like good enough; but it

was. Hall, in full cry – an impressive sight – took 5 for 60, and
Australia were all out for 217. The West Indies took a grip of
things in their second innings and with Hunte, Butcher and
Solomon playing the principal parts, scored 373. The mighty
Hall then did it again: he took 4 for 45, Australia were all out
for 216, and had lost by 179 runs.

This was a great psychological boost for Sobers: a winning
captain is usually popular with the members of his team. In the
second Test at Port of Spain, the West Indies were given a
surprise when Bobby Simpson won the toss and put them in to
bat. Was it that he was apprehensive of what Hall and Griffith
might do in the first hour? This seems unlikely; there was
probably a much more deep-rooted reason, as it is hardly
likely that an Australian side would go on the defensive at the
start of the second match of a series when they were one down.
Whatever the philosophy behind Simpson's decision this slow
wicket produced huge scores. The West Indies scored 429 and
386, Australia 516. Hunte (what a great job he did in this series
as the rock foundation of the innings) with 89, Butcher, a
brilliant 117, and Sobers 69, were the prime architects of the
West Indies successful batting. Their bowlers found the task
infinitely harder as Cowper and Booth hit centuries; now it was
ten to one on a draw. The West Indies batted out the rest of the
match as the game was sapped of its interest.

At Georgetown things were very different, in a contest
enveloped in white-hot controversy. On the eve of the start,
Kippin, one of the West Indies most experienced umpires,
withdrew, apparently on the insistence of the local Umpires
Association, which objected to the appointment of Jordan of
Barbados. The association was angry because both umpires
were not Guianese. The game was seriously threatened by this
attitude – an unhappy and unique situation. It was settled by
the appointment of Gerry Gomez, who had not previously
umpired a first-class match, although he held an umpiring
certificate. Gomez, a fine cricketer, thus established a different
type of record, which must surely stand unchallenged for all
time – the first match he umpired in his life was a Test Match
and, even more unique, was the fact that he was a selector for

one of the competing teams. What sort of a job he made of it is reflected in that fact that although another umpire arrived from Trinidad in good time, Gomez stood until the end. His first job was to order the creases to be re-marked, and consequently the game started ten minutes late. Perhaps even more remarkable still was the fact that at the end of each day, Gomez continued to give his radio summaries on the play, so here he was – umpire, Test selector, attending Board of Control meetings during the game, and radio commentator. There surely can have been nothing like it since W.S. Gilbert created the character of Pooh-Bah in *The Mikado*. Why did Bobby Simpson agree? Probably because he was so fed up with it all that he would have agreed to Nat King Cole or Louis Armstrong being appointed umpire! Gomez's umpiring, however, was absolutely beyond reproach; he didn't put a foot wrong as Australia gave one of their poorest Test Match performances ever.

The West Indies scored 355, a piece of flashing brilliance by Kanhai giving the innings its sparkle. Australia's innings had nothing to piece it together and lacked anything positive. The side was all out for 179, giving the West Indies a substantial lead. The West Indies, in their turn, batted badly. For the first part of their innings they crawled along at a snail's pace; the second half was gay abandon, both with the same result – nothing much! They were all out for 180, leaving Australia to make 357 to win. At 88 for 1 the Australians were in with some sort of a chance when tea was taken. However, it seems the West Indies concocted some strategic plan during the interval and Lance Gibbs immediately changed ends. It proved to be a piece of tactical genius. In the space of only fifteen minutes, Gibbs took 4 wickets. At the end of the day Gibbs had taken 5 for 29 in twenty-two overs and Australia had only 1 wicket still standing. Gibbs gobbled that up with his second ball next morning – and the experts said, 'Don't blame the pitch.' It was a masterpiece of bowling and an example of rank bad batting, and the West Indies won by 212 runs. They could not now lose the series, and after the extraordinary fourth Test in Barbados they were surely bound to win it.

It will suffice to list the prodigious run-scoring feats in the Barbados match: Australia 650 for 6 declared (Lawry 210, Simpson 201, Cowper 102, O'Neill 51), West Indies 573 (Nurse 201, Kanhai 129, Hunte 75, Sobers 55, Griffith 54); Australia 175 for 4 declared (O'Neill 74 not out, Lawry 58), West Indies 242 for 5 (Hunte 81, Davis 68). Two bowlers, Griffith and Philpott, each had over 100 runs scored off them in an innings without taking a wicket. It was that sort of pitch.

This fourth Test at least showed that the Australians, even though they were now beaten in the series, were still full of fight. This they confirmed by winning the last Test at Port of Spain. And they won it with three whole days to spare. On a wicket upon which the ball often tended to keep low, Kanhai's batting was again one of sustained brilliance. He hit 121, but only he in the first innings, and the ever-consistent Hunte in the second, offered any sort of resistance to Hawke and McKenzie. Hunte batted throughout the second innings to wage a single-handed battle with a high degree of skill and courage. The West Indies scored 224 and 131 and were beaten by 10 wickets, the Australian totals being 294 and 63 for 0. It had been a good series despite the various controversies. The West Indies, now described as World Champions, were full value for money.

The winter of 1965–6 was particularly important to West Indies cricket although they had no tour. It marked the inauguration of the Shell Shield, sponsored by Shell Oil. The problem which had always confronted domestic cricket in the West Indies was the immense distances separating the various islands. Tournaments, therefore, have usually been financial failures in a community where cricket has never boasted economic stability. Yet the necessity to maintain inter-island competition was absolutely vital to the needs of Test selection. Until 1963–4 the countries had either met at one centre and played a knock-out tournament, or two countries had held private two-match series, or two matches had been played at different venues simultaneously. The triangular knock-out tournament comprising Barbados, Trinidad and British Guiana was inaugurated in 1892–3 (distant Jamaica not competing) and continued up until the outbreak of war in 1939. It was not resumed afterwards. In 1956–7, for the first time, all four major countries met in a knock-out tournament held at Georgetown. British Guiana beat Barbados in their first innings. In 1961–2 a fifth team, Leeward and Windward Islands, competed in this tournament held in Georgetown. British Guiana beat Barbados by 4 wickets. In 1963–4, for the first time, a tournament was staged in more than two centres, the four major countries meeting each other once, in a League Championship, with the six matches being divided equally between Bridgetown, Port of Spain and Georgetown. It was won by British Guiana. Then, in 1965–6, came the much-needed infusion of sponsored money in the form of a regional League Championship with five teams competing; in the following season the Leeward and Windward Islands separated into two independent teams. Barbados were the first winners. This was a vital step in the development of domestic cricket in the Caribbean.

In the summer of 1966 the West Indies were back in England to inflict similar damage to English cricket as they had done in 1963. They won by three matches to one with one drawn, an exact repeat of the 1963 series result. The touring party was as follows: G. Sobers (captain), C.C. Hunte (vice-captain), D.W. Allan, R.C. Brancker, B.F. Butcher, M.C. Carew, R.A. Cohen, L.R. Gibbs, C.C. Griffith, W.W. Hall, J.L. Hendriks, D.A.J. Holford, R.B. Kanhai, P.D. Lashley, E.D. McMorris, S.M. Nurse, J.S. Solomon. England knew a lot about most of them, except probably Rawle Brancker, a twenty-eight-year-old all-rounder, a left-handed batsman and slow left-arm bowler; Rudolph Cohen, the third fast bowler of the team replacing the injured King; David Holford, a leg-break bowler and lower-order batsman; and Peter Lashley, a left-hand, middle-order batsman with a fancy for aggression. Holford and Lashley were to play in the Tests. The general impression in cricketing circles was that this side was not as good as that in 1963, nor indeed were England, although a wet summer was the root cause of so many drawn games. The basic difference between the two teams can be succinctly summarised in one word: Sobers! For this cricketer extraordinary, the Tests were one triumph after another – as a batsman, bowler, fieldsman and close catcher, and master magician in winning the toss on all five occasions! This was Sobers's golden summer, and tinged with purple too. In the Tests he scored 722 runs with an average of 103·14. His scores were: 161, 46, 163 not out, 3, 94, 174, 81 and 0 (this last showed that even he was capable of human fallibility). He took 20 Test wickets, only one less than Lance Gibbs, the West Indies most successful bowler, and that he was maturing as a captain was obvious to all connoisseurs of cricketing tactics, ploys and diplomacy.

Nurse and Butcher had highly successful tours with Test averages in the 60s, and Kanhai with 40. Jackie Hendriks showed again his undoubted class as a wicket-keeper, and the pasting which England were given in the first Test at Old Trafford seemed to suggest that the title of World Champions for West Indies was not out of place. They won by an innings and 40 runs. Centuries by Hunte and Sobers (135 and 161) paved the way for a score of 484. Lance Gibbs did the rest. This was the first time that England had gone down in a Test Match in three days since they lost to Australia at Leeds in 1938. Admittedly, the West Indies were fortunate to bat on a newly prepared pitch before it began to produce some turn, and the ball did turn quite appreciably, 24 of the 30 wickets to fall being captured by the spin bowlers, 10 of them by Lance Gibbs. Sobers and Holford completed the mixture which produced just about every conceivable variety of spin known to man. Holford, a cousin of Sobers, had a very good first Test Match. England were dismissed for 167 and 277. Colin Milburn, that gay cavalier of cricket, struck down in the prime of his cricketing life by a tragic car accident which caused him the loss of an eye, scored 94 in England's second innings, and Cowdrey 69. But there was little else. The West Indies, it seemed, were sweeping on remorselessly.

Now to Lord's – the Mecca of the Noble Game, a ground on which there were once two ponds, in one of which Steevie, an

employee for forty years, taught himself to swim. Now, cricketers from the distant ends of the earth come as pilgrims to play
and watch and boast with pride that they have done so. Its
atmosphere is unique, its memories everlasting – the shadowy
figures of the great players who have trodden the sacred turf
through more than a century and a half are always there to
kindle the more vivid imaginations. It is small wonder that
playing at Lord's in a big match stirs up emotions and often
inspiration. The records are full of valiant deeds performed
here in the parish of St John's Wood.

In this second Test Match in 1966 two more heroes emerged
and saved a game which was beginning to look irretrievably
lost. The West Indies, 86 runs behind in the first innings, were
95 for 5 in their second, which in effect meant 9 for 5. Hunte,
Carew, Kanhai, Butcher and Nurse had gone. Sobers was
there, and in addition there remained Holford, Allan, Griffith,
Hall and Gibbs. If Sobers stayed – and in his current form there
was every chance that he would – could his partners last long
enough with him to make any sort of a match of it? Sobers was
joined by his young cousin David Holford, and they remained
together for five hours and twenty minutes. At ten minutes to
one on the last day Sobers declared at 369 for 5 after their
partnership had added 274 – Sobers 163, Holford 105. Theirs
was a record fifth-wicket partnership for the West Indies
against England.

The West Indies had set England to make 284 to win in four
hours. Rain lopped an hour off, and what was left was the
innings by which all of us will remember Colin Milburn. On
his first Test appearance at Old Trafford he had scored 94, now
at Lord's he scored 126 not out in an absolute firecracker of an
innings. In three hours he hit seventeen fours and hoisted
Holford, Gibbs and Hall in turn for prodigious sixes. Was this a
modern Alletson? Milburn's repertory included all the proven
strokes, and in addition to these he produced others that were
hard to classify, except that they made the aesthetic senses
tingle with their exhilarating improvisation and power. It had
not been intended that Graveney should bat owing to a badly
bruised right thumb, but he came to the rescue and stayed

with Milburn for the last hour and fifty minutes, in which
between them they added 130. Sometimes Graveney batted
almost one-handed, withdrawing his injured hand as he hit the
ball. England, who did not claim the extra half an hour, fell
87 runs short of their target.

So ended a wonderful game of cricket. The receipts of
£58,000 were then a record for a cricket match in any part of
the world. The West Indies remained one up – with three to
go.

At Trent Bridge they put themselves beyond defeat in the
series. They won by 139 runs. This was Basil Butcher's match;
he scored a superb 209 not out. But it was still a team effort.
Seymour Nurse hit 93 and 53, and Sobers 94 in the second
innings, plus 5 wickets and 5 catches, and shrewd captaincy,
and there was some decisive bowling by Charlie Griffith in
England's second innings, in which he took the wickets of
Boycott, Graveney, D'Oliveira and Snow for 34 runs. In shape
the game closely resembled the match at Lord's. The West
Indies, 90 runs behind in the first innings (it had been 86 at
Lord's), were 65 for 2 in their second. They finished up with
482 for 5 declared. Butcher joined Kanhai at a quarter to three
on the Saturday afternoon, and it was hard grafting. They
scored only 73 in the two and a half hours before close of play.
On the Monday, having dug in, the West Indies produced
heavy artillery: they scored 334 in five and a quarter hours.
Butcher, who had been criticised by some for his ultra-de-
fensive tactics on Saturday, launched himself into the assault
with technical brilliance and flair. He enjoyed the rare distinction of taking part in three successive century stands with
Kanhai, Nurse and Sobers. His partnership with Sobers was
like a hurricane blowing across Trent Bridge. They hit 173 in
two hours.

On the last morning, when England resumed at 30 for no
wicket, it was survival they had in mind, pure and simple; they
needed another 363 to win. They failed and were all out for
253. If anything took the gilt off the West Indies win, it was
excess of bouncers – one, bowled at Underwood, the number 11
batsman, struck him in the mouth. Tradition, and common

sense too, has surely protected tail-end batsmen from this type of attack. But it must not be allowed to sour a creditable win, and a second fight back out of trouble.

At Leeds England were outplayed. The West Indies won by aninnings and 55 runs just after three o'clock on the fourth day with a whole day to spare. Yes, the title World Champions was no exaggeration; they carried it well. What the England selectors thought of the proceedings is best illustrated by the fact that for the next Test they dropped Cowdrey, Milburn, Parks, Titmus and Snow, although Snow did play at the Oval when Price withdrew. This match at Leeds was nothing like the pattern of any of the others. The West Indies batted first and accumulated a massive score, 500 for 9 declared – Nurse 137, Sobers 174. They then bowled England out for 240 and 205 – Sobers 5 for 41 and 3 for 39, and Gibbs, the master-spinner, 6 for 39. What a match for Sobers! Neville Cardus wrote of him at the end of this vintage-Sobers summer:

Garfield St Aubrun Sobers, thirty years old in July 1966 – the most renowned name of any cricketer since Bradman's high noon. He is, in fact, even more famous than Bradman ever was; for he is accomplished in every department of the game, and has exhibited his genius in all climes and conditions. His immense power is concealed, or lightened, to the spectator's eye, by a rhythm which has in it as little obvious propulsion as a movement of music by Mozart.

At the Oval England had nothing to play for except their dignity. This, it seemed, was enough. But in the event they overwhelmed the West Indies just as convincingly as they themselves had been overwhelmed at Leeds. England were captained, for the first time, by Brian Close, and wholesale changes to the team had been made. It was dramatic cricket. A century by Kanhai and 81 by Sobers gave the West Indies a first innings score of 268. England fared disastrously – 166 for 7. Graveney stood alone as all around him fell in disarray, and then, as the West Indies had done before them, England fought a strong rearguard action which ultimately won the battle hands down. A total of 361 runs were added for the last three wickets. Never before in Test cricket had the last three wickets produced as many runs, nor had the last three men scored as much – they made a century and two half centuries respectively. John Murray of Middlesex became only the third number 9 to make a Test century. Graveney was the cornerstone of it all. At his best he is a sculpture of elegance and strength, a beautiful bat. Murray was the perfection of Lord's academic teaching; Higgs and Snow were robust and defiant. Graveney was finally run out for 165. Murray made 112, Higgs 63 and Snow 59 not out. In the West Indies second innings Butcher and Nurse scored 130 out of 225; not enough by a long way. But, all the same, twice in succession had the West Indies beaten England in England by three matches to one. They were still at the peak point their cricket had scaled.

The West Indies followed this success with a short three-match Test series in India in the winter of 1966–7. They won two and drew the other which meant that of their last twenty-three Tests they had won fifteen outright, and lost only three. Yet it was significant that at the end of this tour D. J. Rutnagur wrote in *Wisden:* 'One's immediate estimate at the end of this short tour was that the West Indies had declined in strength. There could be little doubt about the validity of this impression where the great fast-bowling team of Hall and Griffith are concerned.' The years ahead, starved as they were of Test victories, would seem to be ample confirmation of this view. After this Indian tour the West Indies were to play thirty-one Test Matches between 1967–8 and 1972–3, and win only two of them. They were the most barren years in West Indian cricket history. In four successive series involving eighteen matches they failed to win one.

But despite Rutnagur's assessment and its hard core of truth, India presented only minimal problems. As compensation for any West Indian shortcomings was the arrival on the Test scene of Clive Lloyd. He scored 82 and 78 not out in his first Test. Chandra and Venkat were among the first bowlers of the world to receive the full force of this man's extraordinary powers. Rutnagur had been swift to notice another of Lloyd's attributes. 'As a fielder,' he said, 'he was quite outstanding.' He was right!

Sobers continued along his path of triumph. He had a Test average of 114, Kanhai, Lloyd and Hunte all averaged over 50 – and even Charlie Griffith averaged 44. The wicket-takers were Sobers and Gibbs who took 32 wickets between them in the Tests, the combined bowling of Griffith, Holford, Hall and Lloyd achieving only 24 dismissals.

The West Indies won the first Test by 6 wickets. Borde scored 121 of India's first innings total of 296. The West Indies replied with 421 (Hunte 101, Lloyd 82, Holford 80, Sobers 50, Hendriks 48). India 217 for 8 in their second innings, staged a magnificent rally – Kunderan making 79 and Venkat 26 – and their final total of 316 set the West Indies 192 to win. This they accomplished for the loss of 4 wickets.

At Calcutta, the West Indies won the second Test with consummate ease – by an innings and 45 runs. It will not, however, be remembered for its cricket so much as for a riot which all but caused the abandonment of the match. The authorities had sold more tickets than there were seats and trouble inevitably brewed. The constabulary mounted a baton charge, the crowd launched a counter-attack, and, when the outnumbered police fled, the crowd burnt down the stand and furniture. It was a terrifying scene; players were concerned for their own safety and were reluctant to continue the match, and only when assurances were received at government level did they resume play. The pitch was underprepared and the toss virtually settled the match. The West Indies scored 390, India 167 and 178. Sobers, in his two spinning styles, and Gibbs, with his unique brand of off-spin, did the damage.

The third Test at Madras was drawn. It was memorable for Farokh Engineer, who came within 6 runs of being the first player to score a century before lunch for India. He scored 109 and Borde 125 in a total of 404, which the West Indies passed by 2 runs (Sobers 95, Kanhai 77). India scored 323 in their second innings, leaving the West Indies to make 322 for victory in four and a half hours. They were 270 for 7 when stumps were

drawn, of which Sobers – a true cricket machine – had scored
74 not out.

So ended a golden run for West Indies cricket, and now begin
the barren years. There were four more series left in the sixties
and a total of sixteen Tests. Against England the West Indies
were beaten one-nil with four drawn; against Australia the
West Indies were beaten three-one with one drawn; and
against England in a three-match series they were beaten
two-nil with one drawn. So, of these sixteen Tests, West Indies
won two matches only. Failure was to stretch into the seventies,
when for the first time, the West Indies played three consecutive five-match series without winning one Test – before
the tide turned.

The first of the unsuccessful series was against England in
1967–8 when England won the fourth Test after the West
Indies had scored 526 for 7 declared. They had had no hope,
until Sobers declared, and left them to make 215 runs in 165
minutes. England jumped at the chance; it was manna from
heaven. Sobers was widely criticised throughout the Caribbean
for letting England win this game – and, as a result, the series.
Sobers, however, believed that the best way to break the stale-
mate, after three drawn Tests, was to give England a chance –
England were bound to go for the runs and Sobers thought
that that was his best chance of bowling them out, as opposed
to putting the batsmen purely on the defensive. His critics
pointed to the fact that Griffith was injured, and could not
bowl, and Hall had been dropped. The five bowlers used in
an attempt to win the match were Sobers himself, Gibbs,
Rodriguez, Carew and Butcher, on a pitch where 1,000 runs
had already been scored. But captains have to make their
decisions in the heat of battle, not with hindsight. Just how
Sobers felt about it can best be illustrated by his devastating
one-man performance in the last Test, when he was trying to
put matters right!

This tour was a triumph for Cowdrey, who captained
England. His leadership was impeccable even in some nasty

situations – for example, another bottle-throwing episode in the second Test in Jamaica, at a time when England were winning the match. Yet before the tour began, the Chairman of the England selectors, Doug Insole, had told the world that Cowdrey was not the selectors' choice; they wanted Brian Close as captain, but the MCC had ruled him out for some mis-demeanour during the summer. This was hardly a rousing send-off for Cowdrey, but he had the satisfaction of achieving a successful outcome.

With the West Indies opening as favourites, the tour took a thoroughly unpredictable course. England could have won the first two Tests, and had a chance of taking the third. They failed; and they had no chance of winning the fourth until the opportunity was presented to them out of a clear blue Carib-bean sky. Then, in the final Test, the West Indies came within a whisker of saving the series, Sobers doing his damnedest to do so. It was undulating cricket, marred for England only by a terrible boating accident to Fred Titmus, who had lost four toes when his left foot was caught in the propeller of a small boat just before the third Test. Amazingly, he was to come back in later years and play Test cricket again.

For the West Indies, the virtual loss of their great pace pair – Hall and Griffith – was the telling factor. Hall bowled well in Jamaica, but was a shadow of the great player we all knew. Griffith had taken 5 for 69 in the first Test (mainly tail-enders) but was never a real menace. Hall and Griffith between them took 19 Test wickets. Gibbs, on his own, took 20. Now the boot was on the other foot. England had the successful fast bowlers – John Snow, David Brown and Jeff Jones – who between them picked up 55 Test wickets. The West Indies principal run-getters were Sobers, Kanhai, Lloyd and Nurse – Sobers again, in all but one decision a cricketer extraordinary, an inspired genius in his sheer physical capacity to play the game.

England's batsmen were in tremendous form in the first Test at Port of Spain and reached a total of 568 (Barrington 143, Graveney 118, Cowdrey 72, Boycott 68). Clive Lloyd replied with 118 for the West Indies, Kanhai contributing 85 to a score of 363, but it was still not enough to escape the follow-on. At 164 for 2 the West Indies were cruising comfortably towards a draw. Then came high drama. The innings fell to pieces and 164 for 2 became 180 for 8, 6 wickets having gone down in the space of an hour for 16 runs. The drama continued. Boycott, fielding in the unusual position of short square-leg, dropped Hall off Brown. Hall profited, and dropped anchor with Sobers; they spent an hour scoring the 25 to avoid an innings defeat. When the match was safe they made merry, but it had been touch and go.

In Jamaica, until the bottle-throwing riot in mid-afternoon on the fourth day, England had the match running their way. They scored 376 (Cowdrey 101, Edrich 96) and then a magnificent piece of fast bowling by Snow (7 for 49) shot the West Indies out for 143 and inevitably they followed on. The West Indies were 204 for 5 in their second innings – still 29 runs behind England – when the dismissal of Butcher by a diving catch on the leg-side by Parks caused the eruption. Peter Smith, writing in *Cricket Monthly*, commented: 'I have no doubts that, but for the bottle-throwing incidents, England would have won this match comfortably on the fifth day. I am equally certain that, but for the mistaken use of tear-gas which harmed only the many innocent people in the crowd and delayed the clearing-up operations, England would never have been in danger of defeat as they were in the extra 75 minutes on the sixth day! When the players did reappear 95 minutes after the stoppage had begun, England were clearly not the same side.'

An unbeaten century by Sobers enabled the West Indies to declare at 391, and then this bizarre game of cricket, as varied in patterns as a patchwork quilt, ended as melodramatically as anything that had occurred before in the match. England were finally 68 for 8, struggling desperately against the flighted spin of Gibbs and Sobers on a wicket which, from a photograph taken by Pauline Johnston, wife of the BBC commentator Brian Johnston, looked in texture like a jigsaw puzzle – yet it played genuinely enough. So ended one of the most remarkable transformations in the history of Test cricket. The West Indies Board, deeply upset at the events of the fourth day, admitted that final victory for the West Indies would have been an embarrassment to them. Justice was seen to be done. Momentarily – but no more than for a fleeting moment – England appeared to be in a very good position in the third Test in Barbados. With a lead of 100, they had 3 West Indies second innings wickets down for 79, but at this point Clive Lloyd, with 113 not out, and Basil Butcher with 60, sealed the game in a draw.

And so to Port of Spain, the declaration and the controversy that raged up hill and down dale. The West Indies scored 526 for 7 declared (Kanhai 153, Nurse 136) and England 414 (Cowdrey 148). Batting again, the West Indies made 92 for 2 and then quite suddenly, a bolt from the blue – perhaps even a bombshell – Sobers declared. England set course for the 215 target with Boycott and Cowdrey emerging as heroes. The macabre sequel to the story is that Sobers was stoned by youths while entering his hotel in Georgetown on arrival for the final Test – Sobers of all people. He it was who had lifted West Indies cricket to towering heights as no one had ever done before him, and ultimately he received a knighthood for his outstanding contribution to the West Indies and to the game of cricket. These few unruly hooligans shamed and blackened the good name of fair play and common sense. It ought always to be on their conscience.

Sobers's reaction in the match was fierce. He scored 152 and 95 not out, took 3 for 72 and 3 for 53, and had England pinned up against the wall in another gripping finish. There could not have been a more appropriate finale to England's tour of the Caribbean than the sight of ten West Indies fielders crouching on their haunches, arms outstretched, fingers poised, within 2 yards of the bat of England's last man in, Jeff Jones. In unbearable tension Lance Gibbs moved in for the final over. By hook or by crook (not by classical batsmanship!) Jones survived the ordeal. The final score-card read: West Indies 414 (Sobers 152, Kanhai 150) and 264, England 371 (Boycott 116) and 206 for 9. Boycott became only the fourth player to reach 1,000 runs on a tour of the Caribbean. Cowdrey put everything he knew about cricket into the campaign; he grew immensely

in stature as a captain, as a batsman and as an ambassador. It
was a memorable tour.

In the remaining three series in the sixties the West Indies were
to win only two Tests out of eleven, and lose six of them,
beginning in Australia in the winter of 1968–9. They started
this tour in rousing style, by winning the first Test at Brisbane.
From then on, the cracks in a great side were becoming clearly
visible. It happens to all great sides sometime or another.
Australia, on the other hand, were a young and highly efficient
team on the upsurge; the balance of world power was beginning
to shift. For Sobers, this was his first experience as captain of
leading a well-beaten side, and, great virtues that he had, he
could not match Frank Worrell's instinctive powers of leadership, tact and human understanding; but then few men could.
The West Indies batting was sound, but nothing like as spectacular as before. Hall and Griffith took less wickets between
them than either Gibbs or Sobers individually, and Gibbs
found himself almost a stock bowler, operating whether the
conditions for his spin were right or not. He headed the
bowling averages, but his wickets still cost him nearly 40
apiece. Sobers, handicapped by the piece of floating bone in his
left shoulder, was thus prevented from bowling his back-of-the-
hand left-arm spin, representing the loss of a useful piece of
armoury.

   The West Indies seem to have developed a capacity to stage
Test matches that swing to and fro in the balance, spiced with
drama, and with instantaneous and decisive changes of fortune.
In the first Test at Brisbane they scored 296. Australia, after
losing Redpath to Sobers for 0, were 217 for 1 – and then all
out 284. Ian Chappell made 117 and Lawry 105, the next
highest score being 17. Then, with this totally unexpected lead
of 12, the West Indies were 178 for 6 in their second innings
and tilting precariously on the edge, at which point Clive Lloyd
took a hand and scored a brilliant century in a final total of
353. Australia, needing 366 to win, were all out for 240,
Sobers taking 6 for 73. This was the sort of start the West Indies

wanted. They were full of confidence at Melbourne, but surprisingly they were beaten out of sight!

Roy Fredericks, playing in his first Test, saved the West Indies from total disaster. He scored 76 out of 200. McKenzie bowled superbly to take 8 for 71. Australia, 14 for 1, were 312 for 2, 435 for 3 and all out 510. Lawry batted for seven hours and twenty minutes for his 205 and at that point must have reflected with joy upon his own wisdom in putting the West Indies in to bat. McKenzie had extracted every ounce of help out of the wicket; Lawry had played his part as a follow-up. Ian Chappell touched a piece of nostalgia when he was out for 165; it was the thousandth century in all Test cricket and, coincidentally, the identical score to that made by Charles Bannerman in the first ever Test for Australia against England in 1877. The West Indies were put out for 280 and lost by an innings and 30 runs.

The third Test was almost as convincing – 10 wickets this time, Australia again exceeding a score of 500, this time with 118 by Walters. Despite a fighting century by Butcher in the West Indies second innings, Australia needed to make only 42 to win, which Stackpole and Sheahan did without being separated.

The fourth Test at Adelaide was very different. Still Australia made over 500, but in their second innings the West Indies amassed 616 (Butcher 118, Carew 90, Kanhai 80, Holford 80, Sobers 52 – after making 110 in the first innings). Australia, needing 360 to win, were 304 for 3 – then 333 for 9. What an amazing victory this might have been, but Sheahan and Connolly held fast for a draw. So near for the West Indies, yet so far; they had lost the series; had they been able to take this last wicket they would have been level with one to go.

The final Test was another match of mammoth scoring and a mammoth margin of victory for Australia – 382 runs. This time Australia scored 619, which included a superlative innings by Walters of 242, and 151 by Lawry. Walters then got a century in the second innings – 103 – to become the first batsman in Test history to score a double century and a century in the same Test. Redpath also scored a second innings century,

as did Sobers and Nurse for the West Indies at a time when the
West Indies needed 735 to win the match. Not surprisingly,
they failed to reach even the half-way mark.

This had been a strenuous tour, and obviously the players felt
the effects of it as so many sides do when they crossed to New
Zealand, but not, apparently, Seymour Nurse, who announced
before the final Test that he would retire at the end of the tour.
He bade farewell with an innings of 258, a highly spectacular
finale. The tour ended one each with one drawn.

Nurse began with 95 and 168 in the first Test at Auckland,
which the West Indies won by 5 wickets. The scores were:
New Zealand 323 (Taylor 124) and 297 for 8 declared, West
Indies 276 (Carew 109, Nurse 95) and 348 for 5 (Nurse 168,
Butcher 78 not out). Taylor reached three figures in eighty-six
minutes, the fifth fastest of all Test centuries, and in his 124 he
hit five sixes and fourteen fours. Carew's was his maiden Test
century. The West Indies were set to make 345 in five and a
quarter hours. Sobers's decision to put New Zealand in had
been proved right – just!

New Zealand won a memorable victory at Wellington by
6 wickets. Dowling did as Sobers had done at Auckland; he
won the toss and put the opponents in. The West Indies were
181 for 7 before Hendriks, Griffith (in place of the injured Hall)
and Edwards effected a substantial recovery, pushing the final
score to 297. New Zealand got within a handful of this total in
making 282. Then came the turning-point. Only Butcher and
Sobers were able to withstand – and then only modestly – the
bowling of Motz, Cunis and Yuille. The West Indies were
dismissed for 148. Just before New Zealand set out to score 164
to win, the West Indies team to tour England was announced.
Griffith and Edwards were not included and they proceeded
to show the selectors the error of their ways with some fast,
hostile and short-pitched bowling that had New Zealand 40 for
3 at close of play. Next morning, however, the pitch was a
little less lively; so, after a while, was the bowling. Hastings
carried New Zealand to a commendable 6-wicket victory,

their fifth in Test cricket, achieved in the nick of time as ominous dark clouds banked up over the ground.

Christchurch belonged to Seymour Nurse, this talented cricketer rounding off a fine career with the crescendo of a rousing symphony reaching its climax. As, Carew apart, no one else made any runs (Nurse 258, Carew 91, out of a total of 417), Nurse was obliged to temper aggression with responsibility. He batted for eight hours, hitting one six and thirty-five fours. Christchurch will long remember Seymour Nurse, a batsman of great quality. Gibbs and Holford got New Zealand out for 217, but Hastings again, this time with an unbeaten century, ensured a draw for the match and the series.

And so to England in the summer of 1969 for a three-match Test series in a split tour. The West Indies occupied the first part of the summer, New Zealand the second. It was a West Indies 'new faces' team; Nurse, Kanhai, Hunte, Hall and Griffith were missing, only Sobers, Gibbs, Butcher, Carew and Hendriks remaining of the side which had come three years earlier. The other eleven were strangers as Test players to the English scene.

One swallow does not make a summer; but for a long span one cricketer had made an enormous difference to the West Indies cricket team, and his name was Garfield Sobers. He probably spent more time in vigorous action during the average cricket match than any other player. But playing virtually twelve months in the year must take its physical and mental toll sooner or later and staleness – a loss of appetite for the game – is a human condition. This, a damaged shoulder, temporary loss of form, and lack of a little bit of luck, all contributed to a poor tour – poor, that is, assessed by the standards which Sobers had set for himself. Previously, in seventy-three Tests, Sobers had rarely ever failed. Now, in three Tests, he scored only 150 runs, with an average of 30. He bowled well, fast, but his wickets still cost him nearly 30 runs apiece. And besides Sobers's lack of runs there was a general shortage – only one Test century was scored and that by Davis, who had been a

disappointment in Australia. John Shepherd, one of the three
newcomers to Test cricket in the first Test at Old Trafford
(Maurice Foster and Vanburn Holder were the other two)
bowled with great courage, but when Sobers broke down in the
Lord's Test he had an excess of work to do, and he himself was
able to take little part in the Headingley Test because of a
strain at the base of his spine. Gibbs found the going very
tough; his 6 Test wickets cost him over 50 each. There was no
Ramadhin and no Valentine now to weave a web of intrigue
around the English batsmen. It was a good tour for Steve
Camacho, and the ever-consistent Basil Butcher, who was
honoured as one of *Wisden*'s five Cricketers of the Year. But
overall, there was not one performance of the calibre that had
enriched the golden days time and time again.

In the first Test England got the best of the weather by
batting first and scoring 413 (Boycott 128). But it was not the
weather which broke the back of the West Indies batting, it
was Snow and Brown, and the West Indies were all out for 147.
Fredericks and Carew did their best to redeem the situation in
the second innings, but after their opening partnership of 92
the batting faltered. Thunderstorms and heavy rain was the
fare for the Monday, and only ninety minutes' play was
possible, but England finished off the match in the course of an
hour on the Tuesday. The West Indies were all out for 275.

The Lord's Test was a battle royal. The West Indies brought
in Camacho, Findlay (to keep wicket) and Shillingford for
Carew, Hendriks and Foster. Camacho, with Fredericks, put
on 106 for the first wicket in the first innings and 73 in the
second. Davis got a century, and Shepherd bowled 43 overs in
England's first innings. For England, John Hampshire scored
107, and became the first Englishman to hit a century on his
Test début at Lord's. H. Graham had accomplished the feat
for Australia in the distant past of 1893. Illingworth, in the
first innings, and Boycott, in the second, also made centuries.

The West Indies, 380 and 295 for 9 declared, set England to
score 332 in five hours and twenty overs, after England had
made 344 in the first innings. In the end, England fell 37 short
of their objective, with 3 wickets still standing. Given the time,

the odds were balanced in favour of England, but there was no certainty about it and the West Indies had come out of the game rather well after the shortcomings of Manchester.

At Headingley, in the third and final Test, it was also touch and go. England won by 30 runs after the West Indies batting had again inexplicably broken down in their first innings. In contrast to Lord's, this was a bowlers' match – Holder, Shepherd and Sobers for the West Indies, Knight and Underwood for England. But one batsman stood head and shoulders above the rest – the imperturbable Basil Butcher, who fell to a disputed catch for 91. Had he stayed, the West Indies would almost certainly have won. England made 223 and 240, the West Indies 161 and 272.

There were two more matches left of the tour after the Test – two triumphs for Roy Fredericks: 168 not out at Leicester and 129 at Southampton. With Carew's 172 not out at Leicester the West Indies were able to declare at 385 for 1. It was a little flourish of defiance at the end of an indifferent tour.

6   New Dawn

West Indies cricket moved into the seventies in the grip of a period of transition. The side of the halcyon days needed rebuilding; it needed success to motivate it; and it needed patience by its followers who had come to expect success at their breakfast table every morning. There was to be no success for them for three more tours. In fact, for the first time in its Test history since 1928, the West Indies played eighteen Test Matches without winning one of them: three against England, at the tail-end of the sixties; five against India in 1970-1, five against New Zealand in 1971-2, and five against Australia in 1972-3. In the summer of 1973, however, the selectors had put the finishing touches to the new West Indies, a side that was to lose only three of the next fifteen Tests, reaching its climax in the golden sunshine of 1975 by winning the Prudential Cup. By then, Gordon Greenidge, Bernard Julien, Keith Boyce, Alvin Kallicharran, Viv Richards and Andy Roberts were household names in a new generation of cricketers from the Caribbean. And there was a new captain, Clive Lloyd. A few of the old masters, notably Rohan Kanhai and Lance Gibbs, were still there – Kanhai, the perennial, who has bloomed now for nearly twenty years, to decorate the cricket grounds of the world. So were Roy Fredericks, Van Holder and Deryck Murray; experience cannot be bought, but it is a vital commodity all the same to tone down the panache, the flamboyancy, the exuberance of youth, without taking away any of its character, or denuding it of its flair.

In the winter of 1970-1 India came to the Caribbean, never having beaten the West Indies in a Test Match, let alone a series. This time they accomplished both, by winning the second Test at Port of Spain by 7 wickets – the only finished

match of the five. Yet, though beaten in this second Test, one
West Indian carved for himself a niche in history. Jack Noreiga,
a thirty-five-year-old off-spinner from Trinidad, who had not
played first-class cricket for eight years when the season began,
took 9 wickets for 95 in India's first innings. This was the first
instance of a West Indian bowler taking more than 8 wickets in
one innings of a Test Match. Noreiga took 17 wickets in the
series and Sobers 12, apart from which the bowling was thin,
but it was said that West Indian wickets generally seemed to be
a good deal slower, or was it that Hall and Griffith had gone?

The West Indies were not short of runs – Davis, Foster, Lewis,
Sobers and Kanhai scored in profusion. The spotlight of fame
was continually on Sunil Gavaskar, whose arrival on the Test
scene for India at twenty-one reawakened memories of Bradman.
He scored 774 runs in the Tests at an average of 154·80. Even
though he missed a number of matches, Gavaskar's aggregate
of runs on the tour had been surpassed only by Hendren and
Sandham. A new star was born.

Gavaskar missed the first Test. Sardesai compensated for this
omission by scoring 212 in India's total of 387, which forced the
West Indies to follow-on after they had been dismissed for 217.
Kanhai with 158 not out, and Sobers with 93, kept India at
bay. At the close West Indies were 385 for 5.

And then to Port of Spain, where India's spinners came to the
fore and the gaily turbaned Bedi, Prasanna and Venkat dis-
patched the West Indies for 214. India, despite the wiles of
Noreiga, scored 352 – Sardesai again being the cornerstone of
the innings with 112. Charlie Davis, now playing his first Test
at home, scored 71 not out and 74 not out, but it did not save the
West Indies. They were all out in the second innings for 261,
setting India to make 124 to win. Gavaskar was in at the death
when India won by 7 wickets. The Taj Mahal was lit up that
night!

In the remaining three Tests, bowlers were shown the way
home on pitches which caused them precious little happiness.
At Georgetown, the West Indies scored 363 and 307 for 3
declared (Davis 125 not out, Sobers 108 not out), and India
376 (Gavaskar 116) and 123 for no wicket (Gavaskar 64,

Mankad 53). At Bridgetown, the West Indies made 501 for 5 declared (Sobers 178 not out) and 180 for 6 declared, and India 347 (Sardesai 150) and 221 for 5 (Gavaskar 117 not out). Finally at Port of Spain, for the second time round, India scored 360 (Gavaskar 124) and 427 (Gavaskar 220 – a century and a double century in the same Test match, which only Doug Walters had done previously) and the West Indies 526 (Davis 105, Sobers 132, Foster 99) and 165 for 8. Gavaskar and Sardesai: West Indians remember them well!

In the following winter New Zealand arrived. In the past, India and New Zealand had almost invariably found the West Indies too much for them. New Zealand were not able to chalk up the same sort of success as India had had, but they still went home unbeaten in an undistinguished series which produced five drawn games. In fact, every first-class match of the tour was a draw; the only loser was the game of cricket. The New Zealanders probably considered it a good performance away from home. For their part, the West Indians must have felt that they had very nearly reached rock bottom – unable to beat New Zealand in five attempts on West Indian soil, which in the days gone by, would have been unthinkable. Perhaps the least said about this tour, the better. Glenn Turner, like Gavaskar before him, performed stirring feats – if at times rather too slowly. He scored four double centuries on the tour, equalling Hendren's record. Bruce Taylor's 27 Test wickets was a noteworthy feat. Once again, the West Indies could get the runs all right, it was the wickets they found harder to achieve. Kallicharran, Lawrence Rowe, Davis, Fredericks and Sobers all scored Test centuries – Rowe making a double century and a century in the same match, a feat now becoming commonplace. Holder was economical; Sobers and Inshan Ali, a fascinating unorthodox left-arm spinner, a trifle too costly. It was none the less encouraging to see a spinning craftsman at work, prehensile fingers and the cunning of a fox.

There were snatches of very good cricket, and it was touch and go once or twice, but the West Indies lacked the resources to drive home one or two clearly won advantages. The results were: first Test, West Indies 508 for 4 declared (Rowe 214, Fredericks 163) and 218 for 3 declared (Rowe 100 not out), New Zealand 386 (after being 108 for 5, Turner 223 not out) and 236 for 6 (Burgess 101); second Test, New Zealand 348 (after being 99 for 6, Congdon 166 not out) and 288 for 3 declared, West Indies 341 and 121 for 5; third Test, West Indies 133 (Taylor 7 for 74) and 564 for 8 (Davis 183, Sobers 142), New Zealand 422 (Congdon 126, Hastings 105); fourth Test, West Indies 365 for 7 declared (Kallicharran 100 not out) and 86 for no wicket, New Zealand 543 for 3 declared (Turner 259, Jarvis 182: this pair participated in an opening partnership of 387, a New Zealand record); fifth Test, West Indies 368 (Kallicharran 101) and 194, New Zealand 162 and 253 for 7. New Zealand fought out of every scrape they were in, and deserve credit for it – that is about as much as can be said.

In 1972–3 the Australians came to the West Indies as the third invader in consecutive seasons. If the West Indies had failed against the two less redoubtable foes, then what now? They failed again, losing two Tests and drawing the other three. Australia won, without any contribution from Lillee and Massie, who had tormented England a few months earlier, and without the services of Mallett, the off-spinner, who was unavailable for the tour. The West Indies, on the other hand, were without Sobers as captain and player. Sobers had not fully recovered from a cartilage operation and Rohan Kanhai took over the leadership. Lillee played in only the first Test and, looking only a shadow of what he had been, spent the rest of the tour seeing specialists in an attempt to get a diagnosis for back trouble. Massie did not make the side at all, yet Australia still possessed the more effective bowling, Walker taking 26 wickets, Hammond 15 and Jenner 13. The redeeming feature for the West Indies was the form of the evergreen Lance Gibbs; he took 26 wickets. Inshan Ali took 10, but at a cost of 47·30 each, and Boyce 9 at 37·77. Elquemedo Willett, a new spinner from Nevis in the Leeward Islands, was tried. He was singularly unfortunate in that the Australians are notoriously good players of spin bowling, but even so, Willett gave them food for thought on one or two occasions and was beguiling to watch.

The first Test in Jamaica, played out on a pitch devoid of a fragment of hope for bowlers, gave the impression that both sides were having a good look at the opposition for future reference. Australia scored 428 for 7 declared and the West Indies tied with them in first innings. It was a happy occasion for Maurice Foster who scored 125 and exerted a firmer grip on his place in the side. Australia, with Stackpole making 142, declared at 260 for 2, and the West Indies were 67 for 3 at the close of play.

At Bridgetown, in the second Test, events ran a parallel course, enough runs being scored in the two first innings to condemn the match to a draw. Australia made 324 (Greg Chappell 106) and 300 for 2 declared (Ian Chappell 106 not out, Walters 102 not out), West Indies 391 (Kanhai 105, Fredericks 98, Deryck Murray 90) and 36 for no wicket.

Port of Spain, however, produced a wonderful Test Match. The margin of victory was 46 runs – representing no more than the difference between winning the toss and losing it. Ian Chappell had won the toss for the third time, yet it still looked as if the West Indies were to snatch a dramatic victory when they were set to score 334 to win on a turning wicket. At lunch on the last day they were 268 for 4, only 65 runs behind and in sight of the victory they so desperately needed. Ian Chappell, whose astute leadership of Australia has been a major contribution in rebuilding a very fine side, continued to attack on all fronts. That is the simple philosophy of his cricket and it carried the day to the chagrin of every living soul in the Caribbean. The West Indies, with ample justification, will point to the absence of Lawrence Rowe as the difference between winning and losing; he damaged the ligaments in his ankle while fielding on the first day, and was not able to bat in either innings. A player who had already scored a double century and a century in the same Test Match could easily have made the handful of runs which decided the issue. The match did at least show that the spark was there for the West

Indies; it just needed to catch fire. Perhaps the turning in the road was not too far away.

It was a spinners' Test Match. This was obvious within half an hour of the start, when Lance Gibbs was bowling to a cluster of short-legs. The spinners, on both sides, took 25 wickets. Walters scored 112 in Australia's first innings of 332. The West Indies were all out for 280. Australia scored 281 in their second innings leaving the West Indies to make 334 to win. At 268 for 4, the home team was in clover – and then Kallicharran, only 9 runs off his century, and looking as safe as houses, was caught at the wicket off the first ball of the afternoon. Lunch had proved to be the change-bowler Australia needed, and sadly the innings died with him.

Australia rubbed salt into the wound in the next Test at Georgetown. They won comprehensively by 10 wickets. There was nothing in it in the first innings, the West Indies scoring 366 (Lloyd 178) and Australia 341 (Ian Chappell 109). The West Indies, now striving to get enough runs to make Australia struggle and anything in the region of 300 would have been good enough on the pitch, aimed for something better, but they overreached themselves. This was batting devoid of responsibility, and pretty poor batting it was. They were shot out by Hammond and Walker for 109, and made Australia's winning task easy; all they needed was 135 runs.

The final Test was an anti-climax and very poorly attended. The sting had gone out of the series, especially as the West Indies had been the losers. There were times when they were in danger of losing this match too. Australia scored 419 for 8 declared and 218 for 7 declared, West Indies 319 and 135 for 5. It was the only one of the five Tests in which no one made a century.

The West Indies arrived in England in the summer of 1973 for a three-match series in the second half of the season (New Zealand having preceded them) with two wins in the last twenty-six Tests, and no win at all in the last eighteen. West Indian cricket had never known such sombre days, but it is a

long lane that has no turning and soon fortune was to smile
again. England were beaten two matches to none, with one
drawn. It seemed likely that the West Indies party under
Rohan Kanhai would lack the services of Sobers, who had
expressed a wish to spend the summer playing for Nottinghamshire, although he did place himself at the disposal of the
West Indian selectors if required for the Test Matches. In the
event he was needed, as was an additional batsman. Steve
Camacho was hit in the face by a fellow West Indian, Andy
Roberts, when playing against Hampshire. As a result, he
underwent an operation for a depressed fracture of the cheek,
and returned home. Rowe, thought to be fit, found that his
injured ankle would not stand up to a long time at the crease,
so he was out. The selectors called on Sobers, and added Ron
Headley to their party. Headley, the son of the famous George
Headley, was then playing for Worcestershire. Headley's inclusion in the first Test was not popular in Jamaica, because
it meant that the unlucky Maurice Foster did not get in, despite
the fact that his innings prior to the Test were 125, 15 not out
and 41 not out. Headley survived for two Tests with very
limited achievement, and Foster was in for the third. Headley
had at least emulated his famous father by playing for the West
Indies.

By the time of the first Test at the Oval the whole West
Indies side, except for Inshan Ali, had been playing English
county cricket. They knew not only the vagaries of English
pitches but England's batsmen as well – their strengths, their
weaknesses. How different from the days when a banana-boat
arrived giving many West Indians their first sight of England
and Englishmen of them. The West Indies had six batsmen
with a Test average of over 40: the remarkable Sobers averaged
76·50, Lloyd 63·50, Fredericks 50·20, Kanhai 44·60, Julien
44 and Kallicharran 42·40. The inspiration among the bowlers
was Keith Boyce; English critics were certain that he had never
bowled faster or more accurately or shown greater ability for
getting the ball to lift off a length. He took 19 wickets, more
than double those of any other West Indian bowler – or
English bowler, too, for that matter, except for Arnold. Boyce

was in full cry in the first Test at the Oval with 5 for 70 and 6 for 77; this was as good a piece of pace bowling as the Oval had seen for some time. The West Indian batsmen had given Boyce a good score so that he had a positive target to bowl for. They made 415, with Lloyd (132) and Kallicharran (80) being the principal run-getters. Boycott alone had the answer to Boyce, Sobers and Julien, scoring 97 of England's 257. Kallicharran and Sobers, with 80 and 51 respectively, contributed to the West Indies second innings total of 255, leaving England the huge target of 414 to win. It was never on the cards, despite a splendid 106 not out by Lancashire's Frank Hayes, playing in his first Test. They were all out for 255 – 159 short of the target. The bells could be rung again in the Caribbean and the rum could flow; the barren years were over and the good times were here again.

The second Test at Edgbaston was something of an anti-climax. It was a poor game of cricket and probably the un-happiest ever played in Britain between England and the West Indies. It culminated in the unprecedented situation of Arthur Fagg, one of England's most respected umpires, refusing to take the field on the Saturday morning. While a hurriedly summoned meeting took place between Fagg, Alec Bedser and Esmond Kentish, the West Indies Manager, Alan Oakman, who was a member of the Warwickshire staff, and a former first-class umpire, took the field at the start of play. Oakman stood for one over and then, a solution reached, Arthur Fagg appeared again. The root of the trouble was a decision which Fagg had given in favour of Boycott. Some West Indian players continued throughout the morning to show dissent, which did them no credit. What would have happened had Frank Worrell been in charge? Well, we will say no more.

What the West Indies had, they intended to hold, and a patient innings of 150 by Fredericks virtually ensured escape from defeat in the series. England, too, were determined to keep the series alive until Lord's, and the inevitable draw resulted. The West Indies scored 327 and 302, England 305 and 182 for 2.

At Lord's the picture changed; the acrimony of Edgbaston had gone. The West Indies, free from defeat in the series, went all out for a win and gave England a hiding and a half. The game is memorable with sinister connotations because the ground had to be cleared of spectators on the Saturday afternoon after a bomb warning which had to be taken seriously in view of recent IRA activities. It proved, thankfully, to be a false alarm. The West Indies mauled the English bowlers savagely, to the tune of 652 for 8 declared – Kanhai 157, Sobers 150 not out, Julien 121. England were demoralised; they scored 233 and 193, to give the West Indies victory by an innings and 226 runs, a margin of defeat for England exceeded only at Brisbane in the 1946–7 tour of Australia. At the end of the Lord's Test, England's captain, Ray Illingworth, admitted: 'We were outbatted, outbowled, and outfielded. There are no excuses.'

Transition for the West Indies was now a past phase. They were very strong favourites when, at the end of this series, the whole entourage moved to the West Indies to continue the battle.

But England's cricketers, like her warriors, often show their teeth in adversity. The series was not a landslide for the West Indies – it was one each, and three drawn. The batting on both sides was powerfully strong, but the two victories, as always, were won by the bowlers. Boyce, Julien and Sobers bowled England out for 131 in the first Test and contrived success for the West Indies. In the final Test, Tony Greig, bowling his acquired variety of spin, as opposed to seam, returned figures of 8 for 86 and 5 for 70 to win the match for England. During the series Greig had been involved in a curious episode with Alvin Kallicharran. In the first Test, Greig fielded the last ball of the day and ran out Kallicharran, who, under the impression that play was over, had already set off for the pavilion. Alan Knott had, apparently, pulled up the stumps before the ball was dead. Greig's action was spontaneous and not deliberate sharp practice, but the effect was devastating, and at a meeting between the West Indies Board and the MCC a compromise was worked out. The appeal was to be withdrawn and Kallicharran was to be allowed to continue his innings. Whether protocol provided for such an amendment to the laws is problematical, but then protocol does not provide for a wicket-keeper pulling up the stumps before play is technically over, and here, the very success of the tour was at stake. It was wise counsel.

The batsman of the series was Lawrence Rowe, who hit 302 in the third Test at Bridgetown. It was the highest innings for the West Indies against England and in making it he hit one six and thirty-six fours. With Kallicharran also a century maker, Rowe added 249 for the second wicket – another West Indies record. Rowe had a magnificent series. His Test scores were: 13, 5 – and then 120, 302, 28, 123 and 25, which gave him an overall average of 88. Kallicharran, the only other West Indian to hit a Test century (he hit two), averaged 56; and Fredericks, even without a century, was consistent enough to average 66. Still, Lance Gibbs took the most wickets with 18, but Julien, with two less, headed the averages, Sobers and Boyce being not far behind. The England side, under Denness, given little chance, had performed extremely well, but Greig's all-round performance – 24 wickets at an average of 22 per wicket, and a batting average of 48 – was a potential threat to Denness's captaincy, which was subsequently proved. Clive Taylor wrote in *Wisden:* 'Greig, one of the game's extroverts, by turns, charmed and enraged the crowds. But whatever he did, he did it 100% in England's cause. He should inspire the side for years to come.'

The scores were as follows: first Test (Port of Spain), England 131 (Boyce 4 for 42) and 392 (Amiss 174), West Indies 392 (Kallicharran 158) and 132 for 3 – West Indies won by 7 wickets; second Test (Kingston), England 353 and 432 for 9 (Amiss 262 not out), West Indies 583 for 9 declared (Rowe 120) – drawn; third Test (Bridgetown), England 395 (Greig 148) and 277 for 7 (Fletcher 129 not out), West Indies 596 for 8 declared (Rowe 302, Kallicharran 119) – drawn; fourth Test (Georgetown), England 448 (Amiss 118, Greig 121), West Indies 198 for 4 – thirteen hours' play was lost owing to rain and the match was drawn; fifth Test (Port of Spain), England 267 (Boycott 99) and 263 (Boycott 112), West Indies 305 (Rowe

123, Greig 8 for 86) and 199 (Greig 5 for 70) – England won by 26 runs.

Before the Prudential Cup the West Indies embarked on a tour of India and Pakistan. The Indian tour took a dramatic turn. The West Indies won the first two Tests, but the Calcutta and Madras matches which followed are now part of India's cricketing history. India won both matches to level the scores, only for the West Indies to snatch the final Test and an absorbing series. This was Clive Lloyd's first tour as captain. It was Test baptism for Gordon Greenidge and Viv Richards, and it was a tour of striking success for Andy Roberts with 32 Test wickets at an average of 18·28. Lloyd's batting seemed to burgeon even more with the added responsibility of captaincy. Against India he had a batting average of 79·50 – Kallicharran and Richards were both in the 50s. Roberts, Holder and Gibbs took 70 wickets between them. But they all had to fight hard against a very spirited Indian side. Greenidge had a memorable first Test. He was only 7 runs short of a century in each innings on his début – run out 93, and 107. With Engineer and Mansur Ali Khan unable to bat in their second innings, India were overwhelmed in this first Test in which the West Indies scored 289 (Kallicharran 124, Greenidge 93) and 356 for 6 declared (Lloyd 163, Greenidge 107), against India's 260 and 118. The West Indies won by 267 runs.

At New Delhi, in the second Test, the visiting side was even more dominating. India made 220 and 256 (Gibbs 6 for 76), West Indies 493 (Richards 192 not out), the West Indies winning by an innings and 17 runs.

In the third Test India were 32 for 3, already two down. The West Indies, it seemed, were well on the way to clinching the series. In the end, Bedi and Chandra were spinning a tale of success. The West Indies, almost half-way to their victory target of 310 with only 3 wickets down, lost six of their remaining seven batsmen to the Indian spinners and were beaten by 85 runs. Fredericks's valiant century in the first innings on a difficult pitch had been in vain. The scores were: India 233

(Roberts 5 for 50) and 316 (Viswanath 139), West Indies 240 (Fredericks 100) and 224.

India, revitalised by this unexpected triumph, did it again at Madras, on a wicket eminently suited to bowlers of all types – the pace of Roberts on the one hand, the spinners on the other. India scored 190 (Viswanath 97 not out, Roberts 7 for 64) and 256 (Roberts 5 for 57), West Indies 192 (Prasanna 5 for 70) and 154 (Prasanna 4 for 41).

At Wankhede Stadium, Bombay, it was the turn of the batsmen, except for a wonderful piece of bowling by Vanburn Holder, which carried the day. The West Indies scored 604 for 6 declared (Lloyd 242 not out, Fredericks 104) and 205 for 3 declared, India 406 (Solkar 102) and 202 (Holder 6 for 39).

In Pakistan, both Tests were drawn. At Lahore Pakistan made 199 (Roberts 5 for 66) and 373 for 7 declared (Mushtaq 123), West Indies 214 (Sarfraz 6 for 89) and 258 for 4 (L. Baichan, in his first Test, 105 not out). At Karachi, in the second Test, Pakistan scored 406 for 8 (Wasim 107 not out, Majid 100) and 256, West Indies 493 (Kallicharran 115, Julien 101) and 1 for 0.

Lord Constantine, MBE

Lord Constantine, yes, and no one deserved this honour more than him, but to the world at large he will always be Learie. The world loved the spontaneous and infectious way in which he played his cricket; they took him to their hearts; and they had enormous admiration not only for his cricket but for what he did for his own people throughout his eminently worthwhile life, and for what he did for mankind.

He died Baron Constantine, of Maraval in Trinidad and Tobago, and of Nelson in the County Palatine of Lancaster, a former Cabinet Minister and High Commissioner of his native Trinidad. He was born at Petit Valley, Diego Martino. He left Petit Valley when he was three or four years old and went to live at Maraval, a few miles from Port of Spain. His father was an overseer on a cocoa estate, and apart from the prime necessities of life, cricket was one of the things he grasped dearly. He and his mother's brother, Victor Pascall, had developed their game to a high standard without coaching. For his part the young Learie, when he was five years old, would get hold of a piece of barrel-stave and, with an orange in the other hand, beg passers-by to bowl to him.

As a cricketer Learie Constantine played with primitive impulses that were strong, exciting and beautiful. As an individual he inspired others, and he was warm and generous-hearted. He cultivated his own personality and became as much a representative of the West Indies as W.G. Grace was of Englishmen or 'Ranji' was of the lands of the Indian continent in the 1890s. He put West Indies cricket on the map, and in doing so pointed the way to a promised land. The way he played it himself helped to shape a culture, showing how West

Indians should develop: they must bowl fast, as every West Indian boy wanted to bowl; they must bat with flair and aggression. Constantine expressed in his every movement – his leaps and bounds as he bowled, his drives and pulls, his cuts and his panther-like springing in the field – the West Indian temperament and way of life. And behind all this vitality was a shrewd intelligence which he applied to his cricket as he did in later years to his high administrative office. He bowled fast – Jack Hobbs vowed that for a few overs with the new ball he was the fastest bowler he had ever faced in his career – but he also had a slower ball, and even a semi-googly. Commentating on his amazing ability in the field, Sir Neville Cardus once suggested that Constantine should have been given first refusal to take a catch sent anywhere!

Learie spent half his life in England, ten years of them with Nelson, in the Lancashire League. Nelson won the Lancashire League eight times in his ten seasons there, and broke the ground attendance record wherever they played in the competition. In 1963, the Freedom of the Borough of Nelson was bestowed upon the man who was then Sir Learie Constantine.

Because of his league engagements, Constantine appeared in comparatively little first-class cricket – not many more than a hundred first-class matches. His Test Match figures (he played in only eighteen Tests) do not bear comparison with those of the great cricketers; he scored 641 runs at an average of 19·42 and took 58 wickets at 30·10. But at Georgetown in 1930, when the West Indies beat England for the first time, it was Constantine who twice bowled out the visiting team, and in his own Port of Spain in 1934–5 he won the match pretty well off his own bat. Anyone who saw him give his astonishing one-man performance against Middlesex at Lord's in 1928 will not think of him in terms of runs scored and wickets taken any more than they count the number of crochets and quavers in a Beethoven symphony. They remember the way he did it, that high voltage of energy that uprooted stumps and scored a century in an hour. His fielding alone stamped him as a cricketer out of the ordinary; he was taught this side of his game by his father, on the cocoa estate at Maraval. Constantine himself wrote: 'I developed an attitude to fielding, and wherever I was standing, I watched the bowler run up, watched him deliver the ball, and as soon as it was in the air, I followed it to the pitch and then watched the batsman's movement, so that my anticipation took me to where the ball was directed or played by the batsman.' His father's philosophy was that every catch dropped added one more player to the other side; four catches dropped meant that you were playing a team of fifteen – and that didn't make sense. Learie Constantine spoke his mind, and as a result he did not escape a brush or two with authority and others. He harboured a certain bitterness because of this, not perhaps without justification, but he mellowed with the passing years and created a wide circle of friends of all denominations. It was gratifying to him to have been able to achieve what he had for his own people. In the all but seventy years of his life he had seen many changes, not only in cricket but in the world itself; changes for the better; changes which a civilised world was bound to make sooner or later. There had been considerable changes since the days when he first walked the streets of Nelson and was viewed with a suspicious curiosity. In the end Nelson accepted him as unconditionally as he accepted Nelson. Cricket had been his way of life; it had taken him great distances since, with a piece of barrel-stave in one hand and an orange in the other, he had beseeched passers-by to bowl to him. His was a life of remarkable achievement.

'The Black Bradman':
George Alphonso Headley

'What can you remember about George Headley?' someone once asked Gubby Allen. 'Just that he was a magnificent player,' replied Gubby, 'and I had very great respect for him.' This, coming from the 'Grey Eminence' of Lord's, was tribute indeed. He went on to tell a story about the Lord's Test of 1933 in which he thought he had had a pretty good match. As he came off the field, an MCC member said to him, 'I suppose you think you have had a good match, Allen, but I hope you realise that you have spoiled it for us by getting George Headley out twice.'

Born in Panama on 30 May 1909, George Headley made
himself a cricketer, instinct showing him the way. If there was a
canon law of cricket he found it by accident and not by design,
or he found it by genius – one or the other. He was comparatively slightly built; in physical make-up he was not unlike
Don Bradman, with the same hawk-eye, the same perfection in
timing, and the same thrusting power off the back foot, all
balance and timing and movement of wrist. He punched the
ball rather than hit it; his strokes did not have the rippling
muscles of Everton Weekes behind them, but the end product
was roughly the same. If he hit wide of a fielder, then the ball
was through for four. There were no half-measures about him;
he was an artist from tip to toe, a beautiful mover, a great
cricketer by classical standards. A panel of experts some years
ago were asked to name the twenty best players of the twentieth
century, the panel consisting of Bradman, Fingleton, Ames and
Allen. All four included George Headley, for he, more than
any other player, will be associated with the emergence of
West Indian cricket, in much the same way as Grace is with
English cricket, whose standards he helped lift through a
period of development into maturity.

In 1927 Headley played his first big cricket for St Catherine
Cricket Club, Jamaica. In 1928, at the age of nineteen, he
scored 211 against Lionel Tennyson's team at Melbourne
Park, Kingston. This was not sufficient however, to earn
him a trip to England with the 1928 team, but it soon became clear that before long a new star of radiant brightness
would grace the international cricket scene. In March 1929
Headley scored 143 against Julien Cahn's team, and in January
1930 in Barbados he made his first appearance in the highest
company, scoring 21 and 176 against England and thus enjoying the distinction of making a century on his first Test appearance for the West Indies. His second Test was a disappointment
but at Georgetown in February 1930 George Headley joined the
very select band of cricket immortals by scoring a century in
each innings of a Test Match. Moreover, he was the prime
architect of the West Indies first win in a Test Match against
England, and in the second innings of the fourth Test Match

Headley crowned his Test début season by hitting 233, batting six hours and scoring twenty-eight fours. His batting average for the series was 87·87 – a genuine average, in the sense that he was out each time in his eight innings. Bradman perhaps excepted, this was one of the most outstanding performances by a cricketer anywhere in the world in a first Test series; here was no ordinary cricketer, no flash in the pan. Bowlers were already asking themselves, 'How do you bowl to him?' His final batting figures in Test cricket were the complete fulfilment of his early promise, and his average of 60·83 still tops the West Indies batting averages. He played in twenty-two Tests, hit 2,190 runs, ten centuries, with a highest score of 270 not out. What his final achievements might have been had the war not cut deep inroads into his career at its prime, is difficult to imagine. Yet, in a way there would surely have been little change, for the mark of greatness is consistency.

In the winter of 1930–1 Headley arrived in Australia with the West Indies team. News of his prowess had preceded him and the Australian cricketing public were highly enthusiastic to see this young player who had been compared in skill to their own Don Bradman. Headley began disastrously in the Tests, his scores in the first two matches being 0 and 11 (Clarrie Grimmett took his wicket each time), and 14 and 2. Bradman's were 4 and 25. Surely, sooner or later, something would happen. It did. In the third Test, Bradman scored 223, and Headley not out 102 in a West Indies total of 193. He went in first wicket down, with 5 runs on the board, and fought single-handed (the next highest score was 21) to the bitter end. In the fifth Test he hit another century in a memorable match for the West Indies, their first defeat of the Australians. Headley had played a dominant role in his team's victory and the Australian critics were unanimous in their opinion that he stood out head and shoulders above his contemporaries in West Indies cricket.

In 1933 Headley came to England. He arrived with a considerable and well-earned reputation, the ace of trumps in the pack. There was no question of his failing; the only question was what would be the precise extent of his success. It was, in the event, a triumphant tour for him. He headed the batting

averages in both the Tests and the first-class games, and during
the season he made seven centuries, his highest score being 224
not out against Somerset. In 38 innings he averaged over 66.
Among the many landmarks was his 129 on his first appearance
at Lord's. The connoisseurs who studied him closely noted that
Headley watched the ball so far on to the bat that it seemed
almost too late for him to make the stroke. What is the lasting
memory of him? Those who played with, and against him,
will tell you that it is, without question, his facility for going
back on the right foot and driving with an exploding force,
placed supremely well between gaps in the field. Weekes,
Worrell, Walcott, Sobers, Lloyd – all of them great players, yet
of all of them George Headley was the forerunner. He set a
West Indian standard for them to emulate; his genius paved
the way.

The Famous 'W' Plan:
Worrell, Weekes and Walcott

Cricket, throughout its long history, has thrown up famous
partnerships: the speed of McDonald and Gregory, Larwood
and Voce, Statham and Trueman, Miller and Lindwall, Hall
and Griffith; the spin combinations of Grimmett and O'Reilly,
Lock and Laker, Ramadhin and Valentine; the opening
partnerships of Hobbs and Sutcliffe, Hutton and Washbrook,
Woodfull and Ponsford; and even special batting associations
like Edrich and Compton. But only once have three batsmen
been bracketed together as if they were one batting unit.
Perhaps it was because each of their names began with 'W'
and rolled easily off the tongue together. One descriptive title
was obvious enough – the 'W' plan. However, even without all
this, Worrell, Weekes and Walcott were a tower of batting
strength; to have a chance of winning you had to get all three
out, so in that sense they were as one attacking force. When we
think of 1950 we automatically divide that great West Indies
side up into combinations – Ramadhin and Valentine, Rae and
Stollmeyer, Worrell, Weekes and Walcott. The impact which
these three splendid batsmen had upon world cricket – and
upon the world's bowlers – is hard to measure; the pleasure

they gave to those who watched them is quite immeasurable. They were different in character and different in style; their cricket was compounded of grace and ruthless ferocity. We shall never see the likes of such a trio again.

Sir Frank Worrell

Sir Frank Worrell once wrote that the island of Barbados, his birth-place, lacked a hero. As usual, he was underplaying himself. Frank Maglinne Worrell was the first hero of the new nation of Barbados and anyone who doubted that had only to be in the island when his body was brought home in mid-March of 1967. Or in Westminster Abbey when West Indians of all backgrounds and shades of opinion paid their last respects to a man who had done more than any other of their countrymen to bind together the new nations of the Carib-bean and establish a reputation for fair play throughout the world. Never before had a cricketer been honoured with a memorial service in Westminster Abbey.

These words were written in the 1968 edition of *Wisden* by Learie Constantine, in a tribute to this great cricketer whose death on 13 March 1967 had shocked the cricketing world and filled it with sorrow. That we mourned a great man was indis-putable. What has perhaps never been fully appreciated from afar is that the distances between the West Indian islands have tended to make them separate entities, and this has applied to their cricket. Frank Worrell, ambassador, leader with a wide human understanding of men, changed all this. He made them as one, welded together in spirit and outlook. Wes Hall once wrote of the captain he admired so profoundly. 'Frank, unlike Clyde Walcott and Everton Weekes, never beat the leather off the ball, but he gave the bowlers less chance of getting him out. People today marvel at the brilliance of Sobers, Dexter and Kanhai, but to me the sight of Worrell piercing the off-side field at the age of thirty-nine, with the same majestic grace and correctness he showed twenty years earlier, put him head and shoulders above the rest. His late cut chopped hard and fine remains as one of the world's greatest strokes.'

His performance as a Test batsman would seem ample

confirmation of the highest possible expressions of opinion of him. He played in fifty-one Tests, scoring 3,860 runs at an average of 49·48 with nine centuries, twenty-two half-centuries and 43 catches; he also took 69 wickets. When half a million Australians lined the streets of Melbourne in their ticker-tape farewell to Frank Worrell and his 1960–1 team they were recognising his great leadership.

The course of Frank's cricketing career was nothing unusual. He was brimming with talent as a precocious youngster and the confidence he had in himself was misinterpreted as conceit and made his days as a schoolboy unhappy. This unhappiness affected him psychologically and tended to alienate his affections for Barbados – and he moved away more than once. But at heart he was Bajan, and would almost certainly have returned there had he lived to enjoy the sunset years of his life.

When Frank was still at school in 1942 he was selected for Barbados. The captain was Tom Pierce, manager of the West Indies team to England in 1957. He regarded the young Worrell as a left-arm spin bowler, not as a batsman. In fact he batted at number 11, scored 30 and was promoted to number 10 in the second innings. Worrell himself has said that the turning-point in his career came in 1943 in a match against Trinidad. He was sent in as night-watchman when a wicket fell about five minutes before the close of play, and he finished up by scoring 64. He had gone in second wicket down and it was decided to keep him as a number 4 batsman for the rest of the series. In the second match Worrell scored 188, the first century of his career. In 1943–4 he played what he himself has referred to as the best innings of his life: he scored 308 not out for Barbados against Trinidad and helped John Goddard to put on 502 for the fourth wicket. In 1945–6 he took part in another massive stand for Barbados against Trinidad – an unbroken partnership of 574 with Clyde Walcott, Worrell scoring 255 not out.

He batted at number 4 in his first Test Match against England in Trinidad on Gubby Allen's 1947–8 tour and was caught Evans, bowled Cranston, for 97. He scored 28 not out in the second innings, 131 not out in the next Test, and 38 in the next.

This meant that in the three Tests he had played four innings, was twice not out and scored 294 runs at an average of 147! It was no small surprise that Worrell immediately received an offer to become the professional for Radcliffe in the Central Lancashire League – and accepted. What a marvellous hatchery league cricket in Lancashire has been for overseas players needing to become acclimatised to English conditions and pitches. When Frank arrived there were enough good players to take on the full England side – and perhaps beat it: Cecil Pepper, Bill Alley, Jock Livingston, Clyde Walcott, Everton Weekes, Ray Lindwall. Frank's best season was in 1951 when he scored 1,000 runs by 28 June in just under a dozen trips to the wicket. He finished the season with seven centuries, 1,694 runs and an average of 112·93.

Frank had a great affection for the people of Radcliffe and they for him. He married his wife Velda at Radcliffe and their daughter was born there. The flag above the town hall was flown at half-mast on the day of his death. While he was there he took a course at Manchester University and qualified in economics, his chosen subject. It was to stand him in good stead at the end of his cricket career. During his distinguished cricketing life he seemed to have an extraordinary capacity for sleep; he would sleep through a crisis. Once he was asleep and no one dared wake him, and as he was captain a declaration was delayed as a result. Sometimes he would be asleep when he was next man in, when the average player would be twisting and turning in his seat, watching every ball. It was thought that this was his way of relaxing completely. On reflection, however, it seemed that the dreaded disease of leukaemia which took Frank's life may well have been taking its toll of his strength years before.

Frank Worrell was born on 1 August 1924 at Bankall, St Michael, on the island of Barbados, only a few yards from a cricket ground. He is buried in Barbados, and on my visit there in 1970 I was taken by Peter Short to his grave, set high above the university, and looking out to sea towards the lands which he graced as a player as well as ambassador. He had gone when his life was in full flower. The tributes to him flowed in from all

over the world. Perhaps this one is the one to remember him
by, because of its simplicity and sincerity. It came from
Freddie Trueman, who said: 'He was one of the nicest people I
ever played against.' That, in essence, was Frank Worrell and
how we shall remember him, a knight of cricket.

Everton Weekes

When the world bracketed together Worrell, Weekes and Walcott, they may not have known that the three were very great
friends; they were three musketeers, playing and talking their
cricket together. Everton de Courcy Weekes scored runs in
profusion and with an aggressiveness, a mercilessness that had
the flair and flavour of a boxing-ring. He was a sort of Rocky
Marciano of cricket; neither sportsman ever missed the chance
of a kill. Weekes would never let a bowler off the hook, any
more than Marciano would allow a man he had put down to
get up; both were absolute masters of their profession; both
were crowd-pullers. Weekes was a tremendous hitter of the ball,
and his favourite and probably his most devastating shot was
the square-cut. He could drive too, with considerable force, and
he could hook any ball that was hookable. It was the perfection
of his timing and the flexibility and power of his wrists in the
cut that produced absolute certainty of successful execution of
the shot.

If he had a tough exterior – and his cricket, by its very nature,
showed that he did have one – Everton Weekes was, nevertheless, a typically light-hearted West Indian with a wry sense of
humour. He had a fine tenor voice and could possibly have
made singing his career but for his total devotion to cricket,
and was an excellent bridge player, alert to every single card
that had gone. In his youth he was, like Walcott, a very
capable wicket-keeper.

Everton began his cricket, as most West Indians do, virtually
in the cradle. Born in Bridgetown, Barbados, he is a cousin of
Kenneth Weekes, the left-handed batsman of the 1939 tour. He
played for the St Leonards School side at the age of twelve. His
obvious natural ability – he was never coached – first aroused
interest during the war years when he served with the Barbados

battalion of the Caribbean Regiment. He was spotted by
E.L.G. Hoad and, as an opening batsman, made his début for
Barbados at the age of eighteen.

To English followers the comparative failure of Weekes on
the 1957 tour after his brilliance in 1950 was something of a
puzzle. He had a tragic tour, plagued with sinus. This caused
him much pain and difficulty in breathing, and though he always
denied that his eyesight was affected by the affliction, others –
those who knew that he would make light of any handicap –
were not so sure.

When Everton Weekes came to England in 1950 an impressive record preceded him; he had played in all four Tests
against England in 1947–8, making 141 in the last at Kingston.
As he followed this with 128 (New Delhi), 194 (Bombay), and
162 and 101 (Calcutta) in the first three Tests on the Indian
tour in 1948–9, he set up a new world record with five successive Test centuries. In his next Test innings he was run out for
90. In all the first-class matches on that tour he scored 1,350 runs
for an average of 90; and in the Tests he made 779 runs,
averaging 111·28. In 1949, playing for Bacup, he broke the
Lancashire League record by scoring 1,470 runs, and playing
one innings of 195. He also took 70 wickets, though he was
rarely seen bowling in first-class cricket. It was difficult to
conceive that, with this record, he would not score runs plenti-
fully in England in the summer of 1950. The pitches, of course,
would not be as fast and a predominantly wet summer would be
the real test. You are not a cricketer, the old hands say, until
you have proved your skill on English pitches and in English
conditions where the atmosphere can make the ball swing quite
appreciably and disconcertingly.

It proved to be a comparatively wet summer, a challenge to
Weekes' versatility. The result of that challenge was an overall
aggregate of runs for the tour of 2,310, with an average of
79·65, and in the Tests an average of 56·33. He made one
treble century (against Cambridge University), four double
centuries, 279 *v.* Nottinghamshire at Trent Bridge, 246 not out
v. Hampshire at Southampton, 232 *v.* Surrey at the Oval, and
200 not out *v.* Leicestershire at Leicester, and two centuries,

147 *v.* Glamorgan at Swansea, and 129 *v.* England at Trent
Bridge. The 'W' plan between them hit a treble century, six
double centuries and thirteen centuries. English cricket
writers compared Weekes to Hammond as a slip-catcher. It
was a memorable tour both for him and those who watched him
in action; dynamic action it was, and marvellous cricket by any
standards.

By the end of the summer Weekes had equalled George
Headley's record of seven centuries on an English tour, and was
only 10 runs short of Headley's aggregate for the 1933 tour,
though he had played fewer innings. That was the beginning
of a tortuous time for the bowlers of the world. This quiet man
burst into non-stop action as soon as he had a cricket bat in his
hand and wielded it like an attacking sword, leaving a mass of
statistical achievements in his wake – a wonderful player, to be
sure.

Clyde Walcott

When the 1950 West Indies side came to England Clyde
Walcott was bracketed with Don Tallon of Australia as the
leading wicket-keeper batsman of the day. Walcott was indeed
a fine wicket-keeper – surprising, perhaps, for a man so powerfully built, for one tends to think of wicket-keepers as small men,
of the stature of Alan Knott, Godfrey Evans and Deryck
Murray. For one thing they can reach to the ground nicely, for
the journey is so much shorter. But Walcott's size did not
appear to interfere with his agility and he was quicker on his
feet than most men with his framework. In his youth he had
been a better than average soccer player, and could do even
time for the 100 yards. But it was as a batsman that he became
world famous. Few men have been able to hit a ball with such
power and accuracy off the back foot; he employed a kind
of punching action. His favourite shot was probably the hook,
but unlike his contemporaries in the top flight as batsmen he
did not hook square or fine. His timing was so perfect, and his
love of shots in front of the wicket so strong, that he nearly
always pulled the ball forwards, so his hook shots went anywhere between square-leg and mid-wicket. If one was bounced

at him it got the full treatment, and if a slow bowler pushed one through a bit quicker he was on to it in a flash, as if to tell the bowler that that one was a waste of time too!

His Test record is just as impressive as his two Barbadian colleagues, Worrell and Weekes. Walcott played in forty-four Tests, scored 3,798 runs (only 62 behind Worrell), at an average of 56·68 (better than Worrell), scored fifteen Test centuries (only Sobers has scored more), fourteen half-centuries, took 54 catches and stumped 11. For good measure, he also bowled, and took 11 Test wickets.

These were prodigous feats. They were achieved by yet another player who received no coaching: all Walcott can remember is receiving some advice from the games master at Combermere School where Clyde and Frank Worrell were in the first team at the age of twelve. The same year he went to Harrison College and it was at this time that he decided to take up wicket-keeping; he was having a lean time with the bat and the college were short of a competent wicket-keeper. Progress was swift and on his sixteenth birthday Clyde played his first game for Barbados, against Trinidad in Bridgetown. He went in first and was dismissed for 8 and 0. He scored his first century against British Guiana, 125, in 1944–5, and in 1945–6 he scored 314 not out and with Frank Worrell established the (unbroken) world record of 574 runs for the fourth wicket. He hit a century in his first innings against the MCC in 1947–8, and played in all four Tests, achieving 7 dismissals in the last at Kingston. In India in 1948–9 he made the first Test century of the tour – 152 at New Delhi.

When he came to England in 1957 Clyde Walcott had strong claims to being hailed as the best batsman in the world, his record in the previous three Test rubbers substantiating that claim: 457 runs (average 76·16) *v.* India in 1952–3; 698 runs (average 87·25) *v.* England in 1953–4; and 827 runs (average 82·70) *v.* Australia in 1954–5. He had scored ten centuries in his previous twelve Tests, five of them (a record) against Australia when he twice scored two centuries in a match in the rubber. Clyde Walcott too, like Worrell and Weekes, had his spell in the Lancashire League, with Enfield. Standing 6 feet

2 inches, and weighing round about fifteen stone, Clyde had an imposing presence both at the wicket and off the field. He remains modest and quietly spoken, unchanged by the glamour of the world's spotlight. When he laid down his wicket-keeper's gloves he became a specialist slip-fielder and with his long reach and remarkable agility very little escaped him.

Like that of Everton Weekes, Walcott's tour of England in 1957 was clouded with a certain amount of disappointment – not through loss of form, but because he strained a leg-muscle when batting beautifully in the first Test at Edgbaston, and for some weeks laboured under this handicap. However, against the counties in May and August he looked as good as ever. In fact he finished fifth in the full season's averages in England, only May, Worrell, Cowdrey and Graveney being above him.

Walcott, as Weekes and Worrell did so convincingly, proved his greatness on the pitches of the world, not only on the shirt-front pitches of the West Indies. It is difficult, in such a glittering career, to measure his greatest performance, but surely it must have been when, facing Australia in 1955–6, he hit a century in each innings of two Tests, against the bowling of Miller, Lindwall, Johnson, Archer, Benaud and Johnston. They surely will testify to Walcott's rich and flowing talents as a cricketer.

'Those two old pals of mine', Ramadhin and Valentine

England, in the summer of 1950, eagerly awaited the arrival of the West Indies touring team. The West Indies had never won a Test Match in England; their batting was powerful; their fast bowling was likely to be a thrusting spearhead; their weakness, on English wickets, was almost certain to be their spin bowling, which was palpably lacking in experience. But now came one of cricket's rudest awakenings. The two unknowns, Ramadhin and Valentine, spun their way to fame, completely upsetting the cream of English batsmanship. The West Indies not only won their first Test on English soil, they won the four-match series by three to one, and every calypso writer in the business was seeking something to rhyme with Ramadhin and Valentine!

Yet these two were as different as chalk and cheese. But then so were Gilbert and Sullivan.

Ramadhin, the youngest player in the team by a few days, nineteen at the start of the tour, was a small man and he bowled wearing his cap, with his sleeves nearly buttoned. It was said that he buttoned his sleeves to make it more difficult to spot the kind of ball he was going to bowl. Valentine, who during the tour found it necessary to wear glasses, had the bearing of a schoolmaster. Ramadhin had been discovered in a little country village in the south of Trinidad by a Barbadian employed by one of the oil companies, who saw this youngster deceiving all the other boys. He was invited to do a job with the same company and eventually jumped into big cricket. He was the mystery bowler, in that he was different from all other known off-break bowlers. He did not cut the ball down with the palm of his hand facing his body, but rather the palm appeared to be thrown at the batsman to whom he was bowling. This opened up an avenue for deception with his leg-break which he mostly rolled. The quicker ball which he pushed through was confusing to the batsman who was trying purely to pick the off-break from the leg-break. Contrary to a lot of cricket talk, Ramadhin did not bowl a googly.

Valentine, on the other hand, was selected on the basis of being a conventional left-hand, leg-break bowler depending on spin and flight for reward. But all great bowlers have hunted in pairs, and the contrast of Ramadhin's bowling proved to be to Valentine's advantage. Batsmen who had become absorbed in trying to fathom the wiles of Ramadhin saw in Valentine some relief from their discomfort. Valentine, however, in order to keep things tight at his end too, quickened his pace, and turned the ball a good deal more with the quickened action, a change in his method of attack which was undoubtedly forced on him by the economy of Ramadhin. Valentine wanted to be as economical, and he sought the best method of achieving it. Sonny Ramadhin would finger the ball with reverence (perhaps he even talked to it) on his short walk back; then a quick wheel, a few paces, and down would go another one. Alfred Valentine was very nearly as quick. Over followed over, and it was as if the bowlers had been wound up and would keep going until the mechanism ran down. Throughout that summer they took 258 first-class wickets, Ramadhin averaging 14·88 runs per wicket and Valentine 17·94. In the Test Matches they took 59 wickets, Valentine averaging 20·42 and Ramadhin 23·23.

Batsmen, over the years, watched every movement that Ramadhin made as he came up to the wicket to bowl, looking for a way of deciding whether the off-break or the leg-break was about to be bowled. Yet it was said that the West Indies team all knew; there was some slight change in the action, and Frank Worrell could often be seen moving in the slips according to what was coming. Cyril Washbrook, who scored two Test centuries against the West Indies in 1950, said that his method of playing Sonny Ramadhin was to treat the lower and quicker delivery as an off-break, and the one that was thrown up a little higher as a leg-break. He said he was not always correct in his judgement, but by and large it must have proved satisfactory. The off-spinner, when the wicket was responsive to spin, turned more sharply than the leg-break, and the off-spinner was the dominant delivery.

Alfred Valentine's line of attack was around middle and off, to outside the off. He was remarkably consistent in length and direction and he had the ability to spin the ball to get sufficient turn every now and again on the best batting wickets to trouble good batsmen. He had prehensile fingers that bore the scars of battle, the wearing away of flesh from the constant spinning. He had been coached in his young days by Jack Mercer, but Mercer prefers to call it 'developed' rather than 'coached', since Valentine had so much natural ability. Mercer writes:

I knew from the first time I saw him bowl that he was a 'winner': and from that time until he came to England he punctually turned up each afternoon with a small case and two old cricket balls. I told him that he must spin it more and I should not be satisfied until I saw his fingers bleeding. A few days later he turned up with two very bright red fingers carrying the little bag. I don't know where he got the red ink from! I saw him in a Trial match bowling an eight-ball over to an established Test batsman who played at the lot and connected once to mid-off, and that on a billiard table wicket. It was the best piece of bowling I ever saw in a very long association with the game.

One interesting aspect of Valentine's bowling was that he never marked the spot at which he started his approach to the wicket; he just walked two or three steps, turned, and bowled.

Before Ramadhin and Valentine were back in England on the 1957 tour the West Indies had played six Test series – at home, and in Australia and New Zealand. They lost more matches than they won but, with the possible exception of the 1954-5 tour to Australia, Ramadhin and Valentine were still among the top wicket-takers and they were awaited in England with great expectations and some apprehension. Overall, they still headed the West Indies bowling averages in all first-class matches. In the Tests, however, the magic proved to have gone. Valentine appeared to lose confidence in himself; he played in the second and third Test matches without taking a wicket, and then it was all over. For some time he had played under the handicap of a recurrent bad spinning finger but, fine bowler that he was, he carried on. He had taken his hundredth Test wicket in the record time of 3 years and 263 days.

Ramadhin suffered heavy punishment in the first Test of 1957 at Birmingham when May and Cowdrey put on 411 in England's second innings after he had tied England up in knots in the first innings by taking 7 for 49. In the second innings, in a marathon stint, the little man bowled ninety-eight overs and took 2 for 179. But there is an aspect to reflect on here. Cowdrey has admitted that even after this innings he could still not spot what was coming; he played each ball on merit. Ramadhin – and there is no more genuine cricketer anywhere – has said that during this great partnership he asked for no less than forty-seven lbw decisions. 'Surely,' says Ramadhin, 'at least one of them must have been out', and he will go to his grave believing this to be true. Cowdrey's method of playing him was to use the forward lunge with the left leg down the wicket, minimising the possibility of being given out leg before wicket. Cowdrey was an elegant player and even his forward lunge was not ungainly, but was he unwittingly setting a fashion, since copied by other players; it certainly has developed to the great detriment of the game.

Ramadhin was bowled into the ground at Edgbaston and it took him a long time to recover; it virtually finished him for that series. But nothing will destroy the Ramadhin–Valentine legend, nor can anyone question their ability as world-class bowlers. 'Sonny' Ramadhin, now running a public house in Oldham, Lancashire, and still playing as a professional in the league, and Alfred Valentine, who I believe is running a garage near Spanish Town, evoke memories of a wonderful summer a quarter of a century ago. It hardly seems possible that twenty-five years have flown by since together they wrote a piece of history – 'those two old pals of mine, Ramadhin and Valentine'.

Sir Garfield Sobers

Critics in the various golden ages of cricket have dared, from time to time, to refer to a player as the greatest player of all time. When they do so, it invariably stirs elder statesmen from another age to deny it. Someone is bound to mention Hammond or Miller when I now describe Sobers as the greatest player of all time, but I do so all the same. He used to be 'Gary', even on the dust-jackets of books he himself had written; latterly, an extra 'r' has crept in to make it 'Garry'. Perhaps this is an additional refinement to go with the knighthood, yet anyone knowing him well will tell you that, one 'r' or two and with or without a knighthood, this great cricketer has never changed one iota in his personality. He is the same warm-hearted, human man; still, perhaps, the boy from Barbados, whose everlasting love of cricket and ability to play it have endeared him to the world. Not always does greatness walk hand in hand with humility, but it does in his case.

Sobers's all-round skill as a cricketer is astonishing: batsman, bowler (fast and slow to order), wicket-keeper if necessary, brilliant slip-field or gully, or anywhere else you care to put him. It is as if a symphony orchestra had one man providing the brass, the strings and the woodwind, and conducting it himself, because of course Sobers was a captain as well.

Unwavering determination to reach the top has been one of the principal ingredients of his success. When he left school he knew that he must take a job which would allow him to play cricket. He was invited to join the police band; it meant going away and learning the bugle, but as it also meant playing cricket for the police team, he found it easy. At fourteen he played for the police team against the Empire and batted against Williams, the West Indies fast bowler. He was hit on the jaw trying to hook. Suddenly this young boy felt that he was now a man; in a strange sort of way it came to him that there was no need to be afraid of anything in cricket, if you are master of yourself. In these early days Garry was a left-arm orthodox leg-spinner, but the boys used to call him a 'roller', because he rolled the ball more than spinning it. At that time he batted at number 9; but he wanted to be a batsman as well, so he practised against fast bowlers without wearing pads or gloves or any protection at all, so as to teach himself how to keep the ball from hitting his body. His batting developed quicker than his bowling. He had no coaching but he studied the techniques of three great Barbadians – Everton Weekes, Frank Worrell and Roy Marshall. When he had made enough big scores for the West Indies to be assured of a place in the team for at least a season or two, Sobers started to work again on his bowling; he wanted to reach the top in every facet of the game. This spirit epitomises the man.

He studied cricket with the intensity of an undergraduate reading at university. He had a lot of trouble, when he first began, with Gupte, the Indian spinner. Gupte used to bowl two types of googlies with an almost identical delivery, so that Sobers had to watch the ball rotating in the air to try and pick it out. That, like all the other problems of cricket, he duly mastered.

Sobers was truly a great artist, lovely and supple to the eye as a batsman, absorbing to watch as he tossed up his spin, and stimulating as he moved in to his delivery stride to bowl fast with a rhythm and body movement that somehow exemplified human endeavour as well as athletic poise and perfection. Like so many of his compatriots, Sobers hit with tremendous force off the back foot. He could play fluently, gracefully, but he still had the temperament to cash in on good batting wickets and accumulated runs with the same greediness that Bradman had shown before him. Some of his huge scores speak for themselves such as the 365 not out for the West Indies against Pakistan in Jamaica in 1957–8, mentioned earlier. A partnership of 446 with Conrad Hunte was the second highest stand in Test cricket, falling only five runs short of the 451 put up by Bradman and Ponsford at the Oval in 1934. These further statistics speak for themselves: Sobers played in ninety-three Test Matches, scoring twenty-six centuries and thirty half-centuries; he has a Test batting average of 57·78, has taken 235 Test wickets and held 110 catches; he was captain in thirty-nine Tests and he played in eighty-five consecutive Tests from the second Test against Australia in 1954–5 to the fifth Test against New Zealand in 1971–2, a record for any country; he has scored more Test runs than any other player and has played in more Tests than any other overseas player; he once hit six sixes in one over for Nottinghamshire against Glamorgan at Swansea in 1968, the first-ever instance of this feat in first-class cricket; he has scored two centuries in a match, twice. He has won four Man of the Match awards in the Gillette Cup; he has played league cricket in England and played for South Australia in the Sheffield Shield. He first played for his native Barbados at the age of sixteen. Had he done something comparable on the field of battle he would surely have won the Victoria Cross at least three times! To chronicle his individual performances in detail would read like a page from a company balance-sheet.

His opponents will remember him as a great competitor as well as a great player. Macaulay once wrote: 'A great man who neither sought nor shunned greatness, who found glory only because glory lay in the plain path of duty.' This could well be an epitaph to Sobers, who believed that he had a duty to his people. He will be revered throughout the cricketing world for the way in which he discharged that duty. As Sir Garfield, Gary or Garry, he will be remembered vividly and affectionately as long as the game of cricket is played.

Wesley Hall

'This nineteen-year-old schoolboy is the surprise "pick" of the team,' wrote an English critic in 1957, but he qualified this remark by adding: 'The success of Ramadhin and Valentine in 1950, however, behoves us to watch him carefully.' At that time Wesley Hall's experience was limited to three matches, but he already held one record – a batting record. With Gerry Alexander he added 134 for the ninth wicket in the second trial match. Hall's contribution was 77 in ninety-two minutes.

Wes never ceased to love his batting even though he became one of the world's great fast bowlers. What a sight he was in full flight, a gold crucifix flashing at his throat as he burned up the grass in covering the 26 yards of his run-up before the delivery stride, all 6 feet 3 inches and 14½ stone of him. It was a springing gallop of a run with all the classic requirements – the left side showing to the batsman, the front of the left shoulder pointing down the wicket, enough to put the fear of God into any but the brave, and even the brave had little relish for the bouncer he bowled so effectively.

Behind these outward signs of aggression which made him such a great competitor lay the personality of a warm-hearted man. He was a comedian who fancied his singing a bit, and loved to get away with the most outrageous runs when he was batting, so ridiculous that the fielding side could not believe that he would dare to steal a run. When they found that Wes had kidded them again, all they could do was to laugh with him.

He would bowl his heart out and blister his feet terribly in the process. Richie Benaud wrote of him: 'My abiding memory of him in his playing days will always be at the Brisbane Cricket Ground on the tied Test final day, bowling that last over of the match, sweat pouring from his brow, crucifix bobbing and glinting, bowling his heart out for Frank Worrell.' Most cricketers would bowl their hearts out for Frank Worrell, and, Wes more than most. He had enormous respect for Frank, sentiments which were reciprocal. Frank wrote of him: 'Wes has revealed himself as a deep thinker. He has made a tremendous contribution to the planning of West Indies cricket, and he has no equal as an entertainer.'

It was on the beaches near Bridgetown, Barbados, that Wesley Hall learned his first painful lessons in cricket. A group of lads, barefooted on the sand, would play from first light until dusk. Running around in deep loose sand slows down your speed but builds up powerful leg muscles – muscles which were to carry Wes along through over after over on the cricket grounds of the world. Yet in those days he had no thought of becoming a fast bowler. Wes was a wicket-keeper batsman. Another Barbados youngster emerging from beach cricket at the time was a promising off-spinner. His name was Charlie Griffith, so had fate not taken a hand the much-feared fast-bowling combination of Hall and Griffith might never have happened.

On leaving Combermere Secondary High School Wes joined the cable office in Bridgetown. One day when he was playing for the cable office against the Wanderers he was buckling up his pads in readiness either to open the batting or keep wicket. But the opening bowler had failed to turn up and his captain asked Wes to take over. 'I have never bowled in my life' was the reply, but there is a first time for everything, and Wes was the sort of character who would have had a go for the world heavyweight boxing title, or tried to climb Everest, rather than let anyone down; so he bowled. He took 6 wickets – and after that he never stopped bowling! What a great service the cable office fast bowler did for West Indies cricket when he failed to appear and Wes was pushed in as the stopgap!

Wes, like many West Indians, had a passion for horses, and a horse nearly ended his cricket career before it began: he was out riding when his mount stumbled on the dusty, rough track and threw him. The result was two broken ankles, a severe handicap for an eleven-year-old. The injuries healed but left him flat-footed and compelled him to wear a special broad-fitting boot; the normal slimline would have burst after a couple of overs. As a kid, Wes had promised himself that if he failed to make the grade at cricket he would become a jockey; at 14½ stone his successes on the turf would have been few and far between!

How fast did he propel a cricket-ball? It was at something

between 80 and 90 miles an hour, and it was estimated that he walked and ran a mile every five overs. In Test cricket he bowled 10,415 balls, which represents nearly 350 miles. In addition, he scored 818 runs, which add up to a few more miles, although the way Wes batted he would have saved his over-worked legs a bit by hitting boundaries. No doubt he is as proud of his highest score in Test cricket, 50 not out, as of his 192 Test wickets in forty-eight Test Matches. It was wonderful bowling whichever way you look at it. Colin Cowdrey, who suffered a broken arm in that never-to-be-forgotten 1963 Test at Lord's, and came out to bat with it in plaster, said recently, with a twinkle in his eye: 'Sometimes I wake up with a start in the middle of the night, my eyes open as wide as they can, peering for Wesley Hall pounding in from the pavilion end at Lord's.'

Whether you have met or played with, or against, Wesley Hall in the West Indies, or in Queensland, in Accrington or Great Chell – and even if he has rattled your ribs a time or two – you cannot but remember this genial giant happily, for he was a true sportsman, a gentleman ... and a very great bowler.

Clive Lloyd

It was in the Sussex captain's room at Hove, on a wet September afternoon in 1975, that I talked to Clive Lloyd about his cricketing career. He had spent the previous half-hour signing autographs through the open window for an ever-increasing gathering of his young admirers. Rain was depriving them of seeing him in action and instead they saw him, close up, as the man he is, a quiet man, considerate to youngsters, his whole demeanour in strong contrast to his belligerence in the heat of battle when he has a cricket bat in his hands, or when he is swooping with those same capacious hands to send a return into the wicket-keeper's gloves, all in one graceful movement, his physical appearance as he does so being a sort of visual manifestation of his play. He plays his cricket as if an instinctive force is driving him. Principle became impulse to him because, like so many of his fellow West Indians, he had no coaching to speak of, and he never tried at any time to watch others as a model. 'I believe in doing things my way,' he says, 'because I know better than anyone else what I can do, and I never worry where my hands and feet are if the ball is at the boundary.' This philosophy has been the cornerstone of all the great West Indians.

Clive Lloyd's career has followed the pattern of his predecessors. He learned to play on pitches which, by their composition, fashioned back-foot players. He came to Haslingden in the Lancashire League for his first experience of the many varieties of English pitches, and playing much of his cricket in England has compelled an adaptation of style but never at the cost of sacrificing natural flair. Now he is in the process of learning the ramifications of captaincy. Deep thinker that he is, he tackles his tactical planning as if he were an undergraduate tackling a subject at university. He is acutely aware of the responsibilities that he shoulders as captain of the West Indies. History has proved that some players have suffered loss of their own form when taking on the burden of captaincy. Clive Lloyd feels that captaincy has added extra responsibility to his cricket and given it lustre – as if lustre had not been there already.

He began his cricket at the back of his home in Georgetown. The whole family played, but only two of them reached the top – Clive Lloyd, and his cousin, Lance Gibbs. He learned to play with older and bigger boys; it was wonderful training and he was in the school team at the age of ten. At fourteen he first played for Demerara Cricket Club and bowled leg-breaks; he made his début for Guyana in 1963–4; and in 1966–7 he was blooded in Test cricket on tour in India. In his first Test match at Bombay, Lloyd scored 82 and 78 not out and the West Indies won by 6 wickets. It was a fine début.

The change from tossing up leg-spin, with all its subtleties, to medium-pace, was forced upon him by the dictates of league cricket. He found no problems with the transition, but his bowling has always been subordinated to his batting, and even to his fielding, but like so many of his breed, he will come on and break up a partnership which has flourished against the front-line attack. As a batsman he has magnetic attraction; he has only to emerge from the pavilion carrying his bat to stir the whole ground, much as the appearance in public of Caruso, or Joe Louis, or Winston Churchill in the dark days of war, used to do. The waiting crowd always cherish great expectations of him, and the greater the occasion, the higher he seems to rise to it, especially at Lord's. The centuries he got in the Gillette Cup final of 1972 and the Prudential Cup final in 1975 must rank with the greatest innings played at Lord's since the first recorded match on the present ground on 22 June 1814.

At the time of writing Clive Lloyd has played in forty-three Test Matches. He has scored 3,082 runs, with a highest score of 242 not out and an average of 44·02, hit seven centuries and fifteen half-centuries. There is no record of the number of batsmen he has thrown out from the cover regions when they have had the temerity to take a run from a ball travelling towards him. This surely must be one of cricket's deficiencies: batting, bowling and catching statistics are recorded for posterity, but great fielding never sees pen put to paper. It is largely anonymous, unheralded and forgotten by the start of the next day's play. Yet fielding wins matches almost as much as batting and bowling. Lloyd in the covers is a revelation; if a batsman contemplates a run when he is fielding the crowd sit up in preparation for electric action. As the batsman wisely retraces his steps to the safety of the crease he has just left, there is a murmur of laughter rippling round the ground as if to say 'We could have told you so!'

While Lloyd received no basic coaching, there are two men whose encouragement and advice he has valued immensely. Their names are Frederick Wills and Berkeley Gaskin. Wills would offer him a few dollars if he made 50 or 100, an appetising carrot to be dangled in front of a young West Indian, and Fred Wills was generous enough to pay up sometimes if he was out in the 90s!

Lancashire certainly knew what they were doing when they signed up Clive Lloyd and he played his first match for them against the Australians in 1968. The previous summer he had played for the Rest of the World, and he did so again in 1968, 1970 and 1971. Clive Lloyd hitting straight, off the back foot, is a sight to behold – from Guyana to Bombay, from Sydney to Southampton, from Wellington, New Zealand, to Worcester, he leaves a trail of memories of wonderful innings played with supple wrists, split-second timing and the power of a sledge-hammer. Yet at one time his sight was impaired when, as a boy, he was struck in the eye by a ruler, which seriously threatened his vision. Happily this was a false alarm at the time, but later on he found that he was not seeing the ball properly and glasses became necessary. He has tried contact lenses, but the dust of the Caribbean caused problems and he has now reverted to spectacles. In no way has his cricket been impaired. Much of his career still lies before him and infinite pleasure for cricket watchers the world over is assured for a few years at any rate. A few records could go by the board by the time this exceptional cricketer plays his final innings, but records matter least of all to him. To play cricket and enjoy it, is his life's dedication.

These are 'The Greats', or just some of them – but where is the line of demarcation between very good and great? Could not Lance Gibbs or Rohan Kanhai be included? Of course they could. What about George Challenor, the founding father of West Indian batsmanship? These, and many others, have all formed an integral piece of this kaleidoscope of Caribbean cricket, cricket which has stirred the world with its vitality, its flair; cricket which, by its very upbringing is different from that of other countries in composition, fashioned as it is by the environment in which it was born and nurtured, and producing dazzling flashes of physical energy. It is seventy-six years since the RMS *Trent* steamed into Southampton bearing the first party of cricketers to come to England from the West Indies, and it is only forty-eight years since the West Indies played their first Test Match. In less than half a century West Indies has become one of the great cricketing nations of the world. It has been a fascinating story of progress and achievement.

8 Prudential Cup and a great victory

In the summer of 1975 cricket launched its most ambitious experiment: a one-day competition at national level with eight countries competing, spread over a fortnight's festival of cricket. The West Indies, in buccaneer style, and driven on by hordes of their own supporters, sealed a wonderful fortnight with a great climax, to be crowned the 'One-Day Kings'. They beat Australia in the final at Lord's on the longest day of the year, 21 June, in a game of cricket which seemed to have gone on from dawn until twilight, and contained one of the finest individual innings ever unfolded on this ground, revealing the real magic of Clive Lloyd. In winning the Prudential Cup, the West Indies used only twelve players. Lance Gibbs played in the first match against Sri Lanka at Old Trafford; Gordon Greenidge replaced him in the second match against Pakistan, and the side remained unchanged for the three other games, which meant that neither Maurice Foster nor Collis King played at all. Since Lance Gibbs bowled only four overs and did not bat against Sri Lanka, it was virtually an eleven-man achievement – and what an eleven!

For the record, the fourteen-man party consisted of the following: C.H. Lloyd (captain), K.D. Boyce, M.L.C. Foster, R.C. Fredericks, L.R. Gibbs, C.G. Greenidge, V.A. Holder, B.D. Julien, A.I. Kallicharran, C. King, R.B. Kanhai, D.L. Murray, I.V.A. Richards, A.M.E. Roberts; team manager, C.L. Walcott.

Clive Lloyd, the skipper, is one of the 'Greats' of West Indies cricket, and in this company is the 'greying master', Rohan Kanhai, a player of both skill and flair, with considerable technical qualities but with the improvisational capacity of the great maestros; he could introduce into the music of cricket a crochet or a quaver that had never been there before and the game would be all the more illuminating for it. Rohan was born at Port Mourant, Berbice, and made his début for British Guiana (now Guyana) in 1954-5, so he has graced the cricket fields of the world for over twenty years. Between 1957, on a tour to England, and 1973-4, Kanhai played in seventy-nine Tests for the West Indies and captained the team for thirteen of them. His statistical achievements speak for themselves, whether in five-day, three-day or one-day cricket. Runs scored are the life-blood of cricket, but the manner of performance remains more vividly etched in memory; Kanhai, methodically reducing an attack to shreds with his full repertoire of glittering strokes, is a cricket gem to treasure.

In addition to Lloyd and Kanhai there were only three other players in this eleven who made their débuts for the West Indies in the sixties – Deryck Murray (1963), Roy Fredericks (1968-9) and Vanburn Holder (1969). The remaining six are all products of the seventies – Keith Boyce (1971), Alvin Kallicharran (1971-2), Bernard Julien (1973), Andy Roberts (1973-4), while Gordon Greenidge and Viv Richards both appeared for the first time in the first Test against India at Bangalore in November 1974.

Deryck Murray is very much an elder statesman in terms of seniority. He has never been a flamboyant wicket-keeper, displaying showmanship and any idiosyncrasies; he just seems to hold every catch that comes his way. Born in Port of Spain, Trinidad, his batting prowess has rescued the West Indies once or twice (rarely in a greater crisis than against Pakistan in this series), and he can also bowl leg-breaks and googlies.

Roy Fredericks, born in Blairmont, Berbice, has all the inbred characteristics of the stylish and aggressive left-handed batsman: he cuts a ball like a flash of lightning, the ball rippling the grass as it speeds to the boundary; and he hooks with a venom that suggests he is angry about something; yet he is a happy cricketer of many talents.

Vanburn Holder, every inch of him a fast bowler's frame, is broad-shouldered and gets his power from the hips – a crescendo of power in his delivery stride. Everything he has goes

into every ball – effort, energy, and a fast bowler's philosophy –
yet Van is a gentle man of whom St Michael, Barbados, his
birthplace, can be justly proud.

Keith Boyce, too, is from Barbados. A Jack-in-the-box
cricketer, he bats, bowls and fields as if every single minute on a
cricket field is a personal challenge to him. When he bowls he is
pretty quick, and at times he can lift sharply off a length.
When he bats he hits the ball a good crack, and in the field he
swoops like a bird of prey and has a fine throw from deep in
the field.

Alvin Kallicharran, like Rohan Kanhai, was born at Port
Mourant, Berbice. Although a left-handed batsman, he obviously has a lot of Kanhai's cricket in his blood; some of the same
aesthetic gifts have rubbed off on him and he plays the game in
the way real cricket should be played. His bat, as if a rapier, is
an implement of aggression and not self-defence.

Bernard Julien is another of the valuable all-rounders whom
the West Indies seem to breed one after another. He is a right-
handed bat and left-arm, quickish bowler. He hails from
Trinidad but is well enough known and admired on the lovely
grounds of Kent, among the rhododendrons at Tunbridge
Wells, or the high cliffs on the Crabble ground at Dover, or the
towering trees and rich foliage at The Mote, Maidstone.

Andy Roberts is the genuine speed-merchant, the West
Indians' antidote to Dennis Lillee. He was born in Antigua and
bowls really fast with a supple action which has a certain
grace of movement. There is nothing quite as stirring as a
really fast bowler hurling himself along the ground from his
bowling-mark, generating power as an aircraft does before
take-off. On a fast wicket Roberts is a decidedly awkward
customer.

The West Indies' two latest innovations, Gordon Greenidge
and Viv Richards, are from Barbados and Antigua respectively.
Greenidge, an opening bat, has shown his worth with Hampshire. Richards is now playing his cricket in the west country
within sight of the Quantocks. A right-handed batsman and an
off-break bowler, he gives the side a nice balance, for it seems
that Lance Gibbs must eventually reach a sunset in a lifetime of

off-spinning – all craft and guile and tantalising spin and flight
that put him in the world class for so long.

The broad outline of the Prudential Cup is that the eight
countries – Australia, East Africa, England, India, New Zealand, Pakistan, Sri Lanka and the West Indies – were divided
into two sections, A and B. Section A consisted of England (the
host nation), East Africa, India and New Zealand, while
section B contained Australia, Pakistan, Sri Lanka and the
West Indies, an unquestionably harder section for the West
Indies than that faced by England. Each side in each section
played the other three teams, receiving four points for a win,
and two for matches which lacked any result because of the
weather (happily, this did not arise in a single instance).
This produced two final tables as follows:

Section A	*P*	*W*	*L*	*Pts*
England	3	3	0	12
New Zealand	3	2	1	8
India	3	1	2	4
East Africa	3	0	3	0

Section B				
West Indies	3	3	0	12
Australia	3	2	1	8
Pakistan	3	1	2	4
Sri Lanka	3	0	3	0

England, New Zealand, the West Indies and Australia thus
went through to the semi-finals, in which Australia beat
England and the West Indies beat New Zealand. And so to the
final. Each match was played over sixty overs, with each
bowler being limited to twelve overs – precisely as for the
Gillette Cup, the first of the one-day sponsored competitions in
England, which must be regarded as the nursery for all that
has followed subsequently.

The West Indies set out on their path of triumph on Saturday,
7 June, at Old Trafford. The opposition was Sri Lanka.
Cricket has a lot of unexpected and dramatic twists and turns
scattered about in its long history, and anything can happen,
but this was surely as near a racing certainty as makes no

difference. Sri Lanka were here to learn, not to conquer, and events ran absolutely true to form. Sri Lanka were 58 for 9, the West Indies battery of fast bowlers ripping the heart out of the batting. Roberts, Julien and Boyce produced a turn of speed the likes of which Sri Lanka had rarely seen before, and it is to their credit that De Silva and Kaluperuma managed to produce something when the innings was dying on its feet. They put on 29 for the last wicket and will no doubt tell the tale for years to come. The West Indies tactical decision to put Sri Lanka in to bat was no doubt based on the fact that Lloyd knew full well that his fast bowlers could breach Sri Lanka's inadequate defences and that early morning was the best time to do it.

Fredericks and Murray might easily have knocked the runs off themselves, but Fredericks was out with the score at 52, and Kallicharran joined Murray to steer the final course for victory. The match ended after fifty-eight overs, instead of the full quota of 120. So at half past three, on an afternoon bathed in sunshine, it was all over, and Manchester folk would have started wending their way home if an exhibition match had not been put on for their entertainment.

Roy Tattersall, the former Lancashire off-break bowler, selected Bernard Julien as the Man of the Match. He shot out Fernando and Tennekoon in his second over, and bowled his twelve-over stint straight through, finishing with 4 wickets for 20 and making Tattersall's selection a comparatively easy one. Holder had been asked to bowl for only an over and a bit, and Gibbs for four overs.

It was almost a trial gallop for everyone concerned. Clive Lloyd neither batted nor bowled, Murray took 4 catches, and the wide difference in class between the two sides was there for all to see. The West Indies merely had to flex their muscles in readiness for Pakistan at Edgbaston on the following Wednesday. Some critics had expressed more than a sneaking feeling that Pakistan could emerge as winners of the Prudential Cup. Whatever the result, it was felt that the West Indies would certainly know they had been in a cricket match.

And what a cricket match it was. The West Indies, it seemed,

had been sunk beyond all trace and when the last pair came
together 64 runs were needed. Admittedly Deryck Murray was
still there, but the possibility of Roberts staying with him, with
the target so far in the distance, seemed remote, forlorn. The
heroics of what followed will remain part of the history of the
Caribbean. Roberts did stay with Murray and together they
inched nearer and nearer to the Pakistan total. Pakistan's
pincer-grip on the match was loosened and, finally, thrown off.
The West Indies, unbelievably, had won a game of cricket that
will be talked about for ever, not just in Birmingham, but in
Barbados and Bahawalpur too – the day that Murray and
Roberts brought West Indies back from the dead. Only at the
end of the day did the pendulum swing sharply. For most of it,
Pakistan were asserting their authority and were favourites to
win. The West Indies did strike an early blow when Kanhai
picked up Sadiq Mohammad off Julien for 7, but Majid Khan
and Zaheer dropped anchor, and when the second wicket fell
at 83 the early danger had passed. Majid, in a white floppy hat
which looked like a relic of bygone days, was in masterly form,
and Zaheer was a useful partner. With these two going well,
anything seemed possible. When Majid went with the score at
140 for 3 in the thirty-seventh over, the match was momentarily
in the balance, but once again Pakistan curbed anxiety, and
with Mushtaq Mohammad, Wasim Raja and Javed Miandad
all making runs, the innings closed after sixty overs at 266
for 7.

It was a very good score, though with the West Indies
powerful batting it was by no means a safe one. Before long it
looked as safe as houses – West Indies were 36 for 3. Fredericks,
Greenidge and Kallicharran had gone, and Kanhai had been
dropped in the bargain. Sarfraz had bowled a splendid opening
spell and picked up all 3 wickets (which rather surprisingly won
him the Man of the Match award in preference to Murray).
The West Indies were apparently in too much of a hurry to get
on with it, and this was not a good piece of batting. It might
have proved disastrous and as it was it imposed all sorts of
restrictions on Clive Lloyd. Although he is temperamentally
suited to any situation and can cut his suit according to his

cloth, his true metier is unfettered attack – and this was not the day for it. He shepherded the West Indies through to 151 for 7. When he went, all hope went with him.

The eighth wicket went down at 166, and Vanburn Holder joined Murray. Holder survived longer than some thought he would, but when he slashed Sarfraz into the covers and Pervez took the catch some people started to leave the ground. The West Indies needed 64 to win. With Roberts's known limitations as a batsman, it simply wasn't on. Yet from being virtually impossible, a West Indies victory began to seem highly improbable, then unlikely, then possible – and all the time just one ball could finish the match.

Tension mounted. Some of the spectators watched and trembled; some couldn't even watch. The remarkable thing was that with emotion spilling over two people on the ground remained as cool as cucumbers – Murray and Roberts. Murray had his head down: he picked up a four when he could; he nudged for a single off his legs when he could; he mustered all his very considerable experience. There was little point, when they were still far from the target, in trying to shield Roberts from the bowling; it would simply have necessitated greater risks and probably resulted in a run-out. No, Roberts had to stand on his own feet, and this he did like a man inspired. He played with a very straight bat, taking runs when they were there for the taking and moving like a shot from a gun every time Murray called him for a run. With four overs to go, 16 runs were needed. Roberts now played a maiden over – three overs to go and still 16 runs from victory. Six runs came in the next over from Asif, leaving 10 runs to win in two overs. Pervez bowled the penultimate over and Roberts failed to score off the first three balls. Had the chance gone, irretrievably? The brave Roberts thumped the next ball straight for four, and then took a single off the last ball of the over. A gripping climax was about to be enacted before a mixture of babbling noise and stony silence (according to which side you supported), but with almost everyone shaking like a leaf.

In their determined efforts to break through, Pakistan had run out of first-line bowlers and Wasim Raja was left to bowl the fateful over. Roberts played the first ball back to the bowler. Off the second a leg-bye was run which was swiftly converted to two from an overthrow. The third was pushed out to square-leg for a couple. The fourth was turned by the imperturbable Roberts to mid-wicket, and the batsmen rushed through like a pair of rabbits for a single – the winning run. Pandemonium broke loose, as well it might. This had been a cricket match and a half. Anderson Montgomery Everton Roberts of Urlings Village Antigua, had done West Indies proud. Without him Deryck Murray could have done nothing and together they wrote a piece of memorable cricket history.

Four days later, at Kennington Oval, the West Indies faced the real test – Australia. The press built this up as a blood match. Would the fast bowlers indulge in a bumper war? Would anybody get hurt? What would happen if they did? Whatever happened, it would be a great match. But as is so often the case in such circumstances, it wasn't. The West Indies battery of fast bowlers dismissed Australia for 192 and a piece of bats-manship by Alvin Kallicharran that radiated Caribbean cul-ture in all its exuberance and gaiety helped the West Indies to cruise home by 7 wickets. Dennis Lillee was manhandled to the tune of 1 for 66 in ten overs; Thomson fizzled out and bowled only six overs. Clive Lloyd said afterwards that it was difficult to judge the real pace of these two bowlers on this sort of wicket, which was no help to pace bowlers, but even so it was a fine performance by the West Indies. They were completely relaxed, as if they were thankful to have come through on Wednesday and knew that the pressure this time could not compare with that at Edgbaston.

They started well, getting rid of McCosker for a duck and Turner for 7. Australia were 21 for 2 and already up against it. At one time it looked as though the innings was disintegrating – 61 for 5, and the first five batsmen out, one to Julien, one to Roberts, two to Boyce, and an amazing run-out. This had been achieved by Greenidge, who, after a spectacular change from left-hand pick-up to right-hand throw, hurled down the wicket to the surprise of Walters. Edwards and Marsh managed to steady the ship at this point and contrived to give the innings modest respectability. They hoisted the score from 61 to 160, but, when Edwards went, the innings petered out, leaving Marsh stranded without a partner. The Australian batting had been poor; the innings had lacked a solid backbone, if indeed it had had any vertebrae at all. All the West Indies bowlers had bowled well and they had fielded magnificently. Their supporters, who seemed to include the entire Caribbean – it could have been Kensington Oval, Barbados – were cock-a-hoop. They were quite certain that their batsman regarded 193 as being well within their compass, whatever Lillee and Thomson managed to hurl at them.

Australia enjoyed a comparatively early success when Walker had Greenidge lbw with the score at 29. But from that point onwards the writing was always on the wall, and Lloyd's decision to put Australia in to bat on winning the toss was paying handsome dividends. Kallicharran toyed with the teeth of the Australian attack, especially Lillee, and even hooked him for six. Fredericks, meantime, was playing a very strong supporting role, as Kallicharran, like a little firecracker, was exploding all round. In one sequence of ten consecutive balls from Lillee he hit 4, 4, 4, 4, 4, 1, 4, 6, 0, 4. The sun, as hot as in Kingston, Jamaica, or Port of Spain, Trinidad, beamed down on some wonderful cricket. When the partnership was finally broken the score had risen to 153 and Australia had lost the match beyond recall. They did at least get both Fredericks and Kallicharran out, but they were beaten without Clive Lloyd having to bat. It had been easier than most people had thought. By virtue of winning, the West Indies ensured that their semi-final game against New Zealand would be on the same ground. Having brushed Australia aside with such aplomb, surely they were unlikely to be unduly troubled by New Zealand.

So, four days later, the West Indies girded their loins for the last hurdle before the final. Clive Lloyd began the proceedings by doing exactly what he had done against Australia: he won the toss and put the opposition in to bat. For one brief moment, when the players came in for lunch, it looked as though he might have been wrong for once. New Zealand were 92 for 1.

Glenn Turner, the most prolific scorer in the competition, had completed a painstaking reconnaissance during the morning, and was expected to launch himself in full sail in the afternoon. Lunch, however, proved to be a highly effective change bowler: 92 for 1 became 139 for 7, and 158 all out. In a flash, a game reasonably poised had been twisted out of all recognition, in favour of the West Indies. Julien took 4 wickets, Roberts 2, and Holder moved in to mop up the tail, clean bowling the last three New Zealand batsmen.

Fredericks went with only 8 runs on the board, but if this produced a ray of hope for New Zealand, it was very short-lived. This time Kallicharran joined Greenidge, and the result was roughly the same as it had been when he had joined Fredericks on the previous Saturday. For a time a 9-wicket win seemed a certainty, but some carelessness crept into the West Indian batting towards the end and the final margin of victory was 5 wickets. Once again Kallicharran held the centre of the stage; once again he won the Man of the Match award; and once again the West Indies had scarcely been troubled.

And so to the final. The sun shone from a clear-blue sky; it had never wavered throughout this festival fortnight as if to confirm that the competition had been accorded a heavenly blessing. Was this match to be a great and lasting showpiece? It was, for it contained one of the truly great innings to be played on that most famous of all cricket grounds – Lord's. But it was not only Clive Lloyd's masterpiece which will for ever linger in the memory. The day, a long day, from first light until dusk, a day of shirt-sleeves, or no shirt at all, and beer queues, and pork-pie queues, with the noise of a bear-garden, was centred on a wonderful game of cricket which produced the highest skills of batting, bowling and fielding, and involved determined effort, especially by Australia in the face of a most daunting and nigh-impossible task – to score 292 to win. There were no tantrums on the field of play, no irritating mannerisms, just twenty-two experts playing cricket to the very best of their very considerable abilities. For posterity's sake, the names of the twenty-two should be recorded, to be revered by generations of cricketers to come.

WEST INDIES: Clive Lloyd (captain), Roy Fredericks, Gordon Greenidge, Alvin Kallicharran, Rohan Kanhai, Viv Richards, Keith Boyce, Bernard Julien, Deryck Murray, Vanburn Holder, Andy Roberts.

AUSTRALIA: Ian Chappell (captain), Rick McCosker, Alan Turner, Greg Chappell, Doug Walters, Rod Marsh, Ross Edwards, Gary Gilmour, Max Walker, Jeff Thomson, Dennis Lillee.

The West Indies began their innings with the cruellest piece of luck imaginable. Fredericks hooked Lillee for a prodigious six, but in the execution of the stroke, trod on his wicket. His opening partner, Greenidge, was soon to follow him back to the pavilion, and when Kallicharran failed, at last, the West Indies were 50 for 3. This was the sort of start Australia had dreamed about. Ian Chappell had put the West Indies in, and here surely was vindication of that tactic. But no tactic means very much if Clive Lloyd is in the frame of mind to knock it to pieces – and in this case he was! Kanhai, himself a stroke-maker of the very top class, merely adopted a watching brief and kept his end going; it must have been a privilege for him to have a close-up view of the vintage package Lloyd unfolded. Lloyd hit 102 in the twenty-four overs he was at the crease, the second 50 off thirty-two balls. The West Indian drums beat out their instinctive rhythms; the bells pealed; and there were noises, too, with precious little semblance of music about them, yet somehow deep down there was a recognisable beat, discernible, perhaps, because everything was music, or had musical connotations. It was that sort of day, Lloyd's was that sort of innings and Lord's was crammed to the seams. The crowd had paid an all-time record for a single day's cricket – £66,400 – and it was worth every penny.

Lloyd, sometimes a hesitant starter, announced his arrival by hooking Lillee for six, the first of two sixes and twelve fours. Then he thumped Lillee off the back foot for four and the day's entertainment had begun. His dismissal, after reaching his century, had all the drama that had characterised his innings from start to finish. Marsh shouted for a catch at the wicket;

Gilmour, the bowler, leapt up towards heaven with his appeal. Bird, the umpire, who was apparently quite certain that Lloyd had touched the ball but not so sure that Marsh had taken a clean catch, walked over to Spencer, at square-leg, for confirmation. Lord's was hushed, an extraordinary chilling silence – and then up went Bird's finger. The two umpires between them had given him out, and 50 for 3 was now 199 for 4.

Kanhai reached 50, Boyce and Julien made some very useful runs and the final score of 291 for 8 looked unassailable. Australia had taken a hammering from which not even their usually reliable fielding escaped: there were dropped catches, the most salient being by Ross Edwards when Lloyd had scored only 26. It had left their batsmen with a Herculean task, but there is no such thing as a draw in one-day cricket, so you may as well be hung for a sheep as a lamb. Australia had to go for it. It was a hard graft for most of the way, and yet in the end they got to within 17 runs of the West Indies score, a superb effort which gave the crowd 565 runs in the day. It was royal cricket. How appropriate that HRH the Duke of Edinburgh, President of the MCC, was there to present the cup.

Australia's innings had been considerably dented by run-outs, one West Indian, Viv Richards, who was the key figure in three of them, hitting the stumps twice. But Australia were to die bravely. Thompson and Lillee fought like tigers at numbers 10 and 11, and with a final flourish of aggression they put on 41 for the last wicket. Here was a day's cricket with a golden thread running through it. The Man of the Match, Clive Lloyd, took the cup for the West Indies – another great moment for cricket in the Caribbean.

West Indies Test Records

TEST MATCH RESULTS up to 30 September 1975

Season	Opponents	Venue	Tests	Won by W.I.	Won by opponents	Drawn
1928	England	England	3	0	3	0
1929–30	England	West Indies	4	1	1	2
1930–1	Australia	Australia	5	1	4	0
1933	England	England	3	0	2	1
1934–5	England	West Indies	4	2	1	1
1939	England	England	3	0	1	2
1947–8	England	West Indies	4	2	0	2
1948–9	India	India	5	1	0	4
1950	England	England	4	3	1	0
1951–2	Australia	Australia	5	1	4	0
1951–2	New Zealand	New Zealand	2	1	0	1
1952–3	India	West Indies	5	1	0	4
1953–4	England	West Indies	5	2	2	1
1954–5	Australia	West Indies	5	0	3	2
1955–6	New Zealand	New Zealand	4	3	1	0
1957	England	England	5	0	3	2
1957–8	Pakistan	West Indies	5	3	1	1
1958–9	India	India	5	3	0	2
1958–9	Pakistan	Pakistan	3	1	2	0
1959–60	England	West Indies	5	0	1	4
1960–1	Australia	Australia	5	1	2	1 (1 tied)
1961–2	India	West Indies	5	5	0	0
1963	England	England	5	3	1	1
1964–5	Australia	West Indies	5	2	1	2
1966	England	England	5	3	1	1
1966–7	India	India	3	2	0	1
1967–8	England	West Indies	5	0	1	4
1968–9	Australia	Australia	5	1	3	1
1968–9	New Zealand	New Zealand	3	1	1	1
1969	England	England	3	0	2	1
1970–1	India	West Indies	5	0	1	4
1971–2	New Zealand	West Indies	5	0	0	5
1972–3	Australia	West Indies	5	0	2	3
1973	England	England	3	2	0	1
1973–4	England	West Indies	5	1	1	3
1974–5	India	India	5	3	2	0
1974–5	Pakistan	Pakistan	2	0	0	2
			158	49	48	60 (1 tied)

1000 RUNS OR MORE IN TEST CRICKET

	Career	Tests	Inngs	N.O.	Runs	H.S.	Avge	100s	50s
G.S. Sobers	1954–5 to 1973–4	93	160	21	8032	365*	57·78	26	30
R.B. Kanhai	1957 to 1973–4	79	137	6	6227	256	47·53	15	28
E.D. Weekes	1947–8 to 1957–8	48	81	5	4455	207	58·61	15	19
F.M. Worrell	1947–8 to 1963	51	87	9	3860	261	49·48	9	22
C.L. Walcott	1947–8 to 1959–60	44	74	7	3798	220	56·68	15	14
C.C. Hunte	1957–8 to 1966–7	44	78	6	3245	260	45·06	8	13
B.F. Butcher	1958–9 to 1969	44	78	6	3104	209*	43·11	7	16
C.H. Lloyd	1966–7 to 1974–5	43	76	6	3082	242*	44·02	7	15
R.C. Fredericks	1968–9 to 1974–5	39	71	4	2741	163	40·91	4	16
S.M. Nurse	1959–60 to 1968–9	29	54	1	2523	258	47·60	6	10
G.A. Headley	1929–30 to 1953–4	22	40	4	2190	270*	60·83	10	5
J.B. Stollmeyer	1939 to 1954–5	32	56	5	2159	160	42·33	4	12
A.I. Kallicharran	1971–2 to 1974–5	22	36	4	1827	158	57·09	6	10
O.G. Smith	1954–5 to 1958–9	26	42	0	1331	168	31·69	4	6
J.S. Solomon	1958–9 to 1964–5	27	46	7	1326	100*	34·00	1	9
C.A. Davis	1969 to 1972–3	15	29	5	1301	183	54·20	4	4
G.E. Gomez	1939 to 1953–4	29	46	5	1243	101	30·31	1	8
L.G. Rowe	1971–2 to 1973–4	12	17	1	1131	302	70·68	5	2
M.C. Carew	1963 to 1971–2	19	36	3	1127	109	34·15	1	5
J.K. Holt	1953–4 to 1958–9	17	31	2	1066	166	36·75	2	5
A.F. Rae	1948–9 to 1952–3	15	24	2	1016	109	46·18	4	4

50 WICKETS OR MORE IN TEST CRICKET

	Career	Tests	Balls	Mdns	Runs	Wkts	Avge	Best Bowling	5 W.I.	10 W.M.
L.R. Gibbs	1957–8 to 1974–5	73	25258	1244	8337	293	28·45	8/38	17	2
G.S. Sobers	1954–5 to 1973–4	93	21599	995	7999	235	34·03	6/73	6	—
W.W. Hall	1958–9 to 1968–9	48	10415	312	5066	192	26·38	7/69	9	1
S. Ramadhin	1950 to 1960–1	43	13939	813	4579	158	28·98	7/49	10	1
A.L. Valentine	1950 to 1961–2	36	12961	789	4215	139	30·32	8/104	8	2
C.C. Griffith	1959–60 to 1968–9	28	5631	177	2683	94	28·54	6/36	5	—
F.M. Worrell	1947–8 to 1963	51	7147	275	2673	69	38·73	7/70	2	—
V.A. Holder	1969 to 1974–5	22	5175	251	1868	62	30·12	6/39	1	—
L.N. Constantine	1928 to 1939	18	3553	125	1746	58	30·10	5/75	2	—
G.E. Gomez	1939 to 1953–4	29	5236	285	1590	58	27·41	7/55	1	1
R. Gilchrist	1957 to 1958–9	13	3227	124	1521	57	26·68	6/55	1	—
K.D. Boyce	1970–1 to 1974–5	17	2843	93	1440	51	28·23	6/77	2	1

RECORD PARTNERSHIPS FOR EACH WICKET IN TEST CRICKET

1st	239	J.B. Stollmeyer and A.F. Rae *v.* India (Madras)	1948–9
2nd	446	C.C. Hunte and G.S. Sobers *v.* Pakistan (Kingston)	1957–8
3rd	338	E.D. Weekes and F.M. Worrell *v.* England (Port of Spain)	1953–4
4th	399	G.S. Sobers and F.M. Worrell *v.* England (Bridgetown)	1959–60
5th	265	S.M. Nurse and G.S. Sobers *v.* England (Leeds)	1966
6th	274†	G.S. Sobers and D.A.J. Holford *v.* England (Lord's)	1966
7th	347	D. Atkinson and C.C. Depeiza *v.* Australia (Bridgetown)	1954–5
8th	124	B.D. Julien and K.D. Boyce *v.* India (New Delhi)	1974–5
9th	122	D.A.J. Holford and J.L. Hendricks *v.* Australia (Adelaide)	1968–9
10th	98†	F.M. Worrell and W.W. Hall *v.* India (Port of Spain)	1961–2